URBAN TRANSPORT DEVELOPMENT
Theory and Practice

About the Authors

I.P. Gautam began his career with the Indian Revenue Service as an Assistant Commissioner of Income Tax and joined Indian Administrative Service in 1986. He has served as Secretary and Principal Secretary, Government of Gujarat, in various departments like Industries, Energy & Petrochemicals, Narmada, Ports & Transport, and Urban Development & Urban Housing etc. He has also served as Director (Finance) of Sardar Sarovar Narmada Project for five years and as the Municipal Commissioner of Rajkot and Ahmedabad.

Gautam spearheaded the implementation of Bus Rapid Transit System (BRTS) in Ahmedabad, one of the first of its kind in the country. His major contributions include power sector reforms, conversion of thousands of auto-rickshaws to CNG, implementing PPP arrangements for the city bus service and BRTS, effective rehabilitation and resettlement of projects-affected people, housing for the urban poor and many innovations in civic management and project financing.

During his tenure as Municipal Commissioner and Chairman of Sabarmati Riverfront Development body and Ahmedabad Janmarg Ltd., nationally famous projects like the Ahmedabad BRTS, Kankaria Lakefront Development and Sabarmati Riverfront Development were completed and the civic body received many international and national awards for its work.

H.M. Shivanand Swamy, an economist and urban and regional planner, has been an educator, researcher, policy adviser and consultant on development planning, specifically on integrated land use — transport planning and design, and urban development management. As an academic, he has been involved in teaching at CEPT University since 1986, and his teaching and research interests are in land use — transport planning, transportation economics and finance.

Prof. Swamy has assisted the cities of Surat and Ahmedabad in evolving their city mobility plans. He has been instrumental in planning and operationalising the Bus Rapid Transit System (BRTS) in Ahmedabad, Surat, Hubli, Dharwad, Indore and provided support to the Union Ministry of Urban Development in evolving planning and design guidelines for BRTS as well as in scaling up of bus-based services in various cities of India.

URBAN TRANSPORT DEVELOPMENT
Theory and Practice

I.P. Gautam
H.M. Shivanand Swamy

CONCEPT PUBLISHING COMPANY PVT. LTD.
NEW DELHI - 110 059

ISBN: 978-93-5594-640-9

First Published 2023

Published and Printed by

Concept Since 1974

Concept Publishing Company Pvt. Ltd.
A/15-16, Commercial Block, Mohan Garden
New Delhi-110059 (India)
T: +91-11-41101460
E: publishing@conceptpub.com, *W*: www.conceptpub.com

Cataloging in Publication--Courtesy: D.K. Agencies (P) Ltd. <docinfo@dkagencies.com>

Gautam, I. P., 1953- **author.**
Urban transport development : theory and practice / I.P. Gautam, H.M. Shivanand Swamy.
pages cm
"This book is an outcome of a Ph.D. research dissertation "Development of Ahmedabad bus rapid transit system: a study of innovations using actor network theory" on which a Ph.D. was undertaken by the first author of the book, Dr. I.P. Gautam with thesecond au thor as adviser, Prof. H.M. Shivanand Swamy, as a part of Doctoral Programme of the CEPT University, Ahmedabad in 2017-18" --Preface.
Includes bibliographical references and index.
ISBN 9789355946409

1. Bus rapid transit--India--Ahmadābād--Design and construction. 2. Urban transportation --Technological innovations--India--Ahmadābād. 3. Urban transportation policy--India--Ahmadābād. 4. Actor-network theory. I. Shivanand Swamy, H. M., author. II. Title.

LCC TL232.G38 2023 | DDC 629.22233095475 23

Foreword

As India urbanises, and witnesses a major demographic transition, huge investments will be needed in a complex urban infrastructure system. Studies and expert committees have assessed that these would range from Rs. 35 trillion to about Rs. 60 trillion over the next 20 years. Transport systems are estimated to consume the lion's share of these investments, as assessed by the Isher Ahluwalia Committee on urban infrastructure. The successful implementation of many of these projects calls for a good understanding of their complexity and the stakeholders involved. Without this, there is a risk of project failure and a real threat of infructuous investments.

While the agglomeration economies of urbanisation enable economic development and a better quality of life, they also bring with it negatives, such as congestion and transport related air pollution. This is largely due to huge increase in personal motor vehicle use. The world has looked upon public transport as the panacea for this problem, with country after country advocating increased investments in public transport systems instead of road widening. India, with its National Urban Transport Policy of 2006, emphatically advocating investments in public transport, is one among these countries.

Traditionally, buses and metro rail systems have been the two primary forms of public transport that cities have adopted to draw people away from personal motor vehicles. However, metro rail systems are very expensive and buses suffer from a poor social image, thereby being able to attract only those who can afford nothing else.

More recently, bus rapid transit (BRT) systems have emerged as an intermediate alternative, being more economical than metro rail systems and more attractive than regular bus services. Pioneered in Brazil and having expanded to other cities in Latin America, BRT systems have spread to other countries, including India. Delhi and Pune were the first two examples in India, closely followed by Ahmedabad.

The challenge with BRT systems is the complexity of their implementation. There are many stakeholders and a variety of concerns that have to be sensitively dealt with. Unlike metro rail systems, which has an interface with the general public only at the station areas, BRT systems interface with them throughout their length. As a result, there are many more stakeholders who get positively or negatively impacted. Each of these stakeholders needs careful management, without which such projects can suffer severely. Proper handling of all these stakeholder concerns is the key success factor in the implementation of BRT systems.

Dr. I.P. Gautam and Prof. Shivanand Swamy, who led the implementation of the BRT system in Ahmedabad, demonstrated how the numerous stakeholders can be managed in a systematic manner, using the Actor-Network Theory. This theory offers a scientific approach to managing many stakeholders and was successfully deployed in Ahmedabad. The Actor-Network Theory is conceptually useful in understanding the development of large technological projects and, specifically, enables:

- an understanding of how social effects are generated as a result of associations between different human and non-human actors,
- an understanding of the role of technology in shaping social processes and, in turn, the design process, and
- an understanding of how the decisions are made involving multiple actors with varying and often conflicting objectives.

It is largely due to this kind of understanding, and a deployment of the ANT approach, that Ahmedabad proved to be a successful example of BRT implementation in India, even as similar projects elsewhere in the country did not succeed. Lessons learnt from Ahmedabad were extremely useful for subsequent cities, resulting in good BRT systems coming up at Indore, Surat and Hubli Dharwad. Ahmedabad also demonstrated the unique example of good political management skills coupled with sound technical competence, with the authors coming together in a perfect combine to deliver a complex project. Their team spirit and mutual respect for each other's strengths helped negotiate the complexity of the project and is an example for others to emulate.

The book highlights several examples of how intractable problems can be dealt with, if handled deftly, firmly and yet with compassion. Some noteworthy examples that have been highlighted are the following:

- How media was won over through a strategy of openness and sharing information

- How the risks of rules of the road were respected by setting examples from high levels,
- How sensitive religious and cultural issues were dealt with through a process of consultation and, when needed, firmness, and
- How a process of extensive consultation with stakeholders helped bring everyone together.

Public policies and public projects are usually very complex and require a good understanding of stakeholder concerns. Sensitive management of such concerns is important for the success of any policy or project. Dr. Gautam and Prof. Swamy's book provides important lessons in this, using the Ahmedabad BRT as a test case. It is a must be read by all project managers and public policy leaders. It should be a prescribed reading in all public policy training institutions that create future public policy leaders and project managers in the country.

I wish the book all success.

Dr. O.P. Agarwal

Dr. O.P. Agarwal was a member of the Indian Administrative Service from 1979 to 2007. He held several positions with the national and state government of Assam including Joint Secretary (Urban Transport) in the national Ministry of Urban Development and Secretary for Transport in the State of Assam. He was the principal author of the National Urban Transport Policy for the country, which was adopted by the Union Cabinet in April 2006 and has remained the key document guiding urban transport investments since then. He has worked in the World Bank for six years as its global Urban Transport Adviser in Washington DC. He was also the CEO of the World Resources institute from June 2017 to September 2022.

He chaired the US Transport Research Boards Committee on Transport in Developing Countries for a period of six years. He has written several papers on urban transport policy and governance issues. His recent book entitled "*Emerging Paradigms in Urban Mobility Planning Financing and implementation*" was published by Elsevier,

He has a PhD in Transport Economics from the Indian Institute of Technology, Delhi. Master's degree in Transportation from the Massachusetts Institute of Technology, USA and a Bachelor's degree in Electrical Engineering from the Indian Institute of Technology Madras.

Preface

Urban issues are increasingly becoming important. There appears to be a direct relation to increasing urban population, migration, increasing workers and infrastructure development. Mass Rapid Transport Systems like the BRTS are considered to be an essential part of the urbanisation process as they not only fulfil the transportation requirements of the urban environment but also direct an effective urbanisation process. In 2006, the Ministry of Urban Development issued the National Urban Transport Policy (NUTP) which listed its implementation objectives as to reduce pollution, promote cleaner technologies, and encourage greater use of public transport as the policies of concern to the Indian urban transport development, apart from other measures. Gujarat is one of the few states where these policies found immediate implementation.

This book is an outcome of a Ph.D. research dissertation "Development of Ahmedabad Bus Rapid Transit System: A Study of Innovations Using Actor Network Theory" on which a Ph.D. was undertaken by the first author of the book, Dr. I.P. Gautam with the second author as adviser, Prof. H.M. Shivanand Swamy, as a part of Doctoral Programme of the CEPT University, Ahmedabad in 2017-18. Actor-Network Theory (ANT) was found appropriate as a framework, which uses concepts like, Translation, Inscription and Distribution of Agencies, helped the first Author to narrate the process of setting up of BRTS in Ahmedabad and also adopted the ANT framework, for further study, analyses and also narrate status of detailed application of concepts for design production and implementation of the BRTS in Ahmedabad from 2006-2012. A copy of Thesis is available with CEPT University library for further reference.

The book argues that conceptualising the idea and identifying the actors involved in the implementation of the concept is important to understand. This analysis when carried out in the context of Actor Network Theory throws up a much nuanced understanding of not only the analytical results but also informs the theory itself. The urban space demands diverse actions to cope with new circumstances. Thus, careful implementation of urban infrastructure is essential for sustainability.

Throughout this research, cooperation, suggestions and advises were received from many people. We convey our sincere gratitude to the then Chief Minister and Chief Secretaries, Secretary, Urban Development Department, Government of Gujarat, Mayors and Municipal Commissioners of Ahmedabad Municipal Corporation, Chairman & Transport Managers of AMTS, Ahmedabad, CMD & Team Janmarg Ltd., Ahmedabad for their permission for this study and also for their valuable support from time to time during the study period of 2011-2015. We also convey our sincere gratitude to CEPT University & Centre of Excellence team of CEPT for their valuable support and also sharing their experiences and relevant information regarding design, production and execution of the BRTS. We are sincerely grateful to GIDB, AUDA, AMC, AMTS, City Police, RTO and Janmarg Limited, Ahmedabad for sharing valuable information and relevant data for study and the book.

Lastly, no analysis is complete. The urban infrastructure programme and implementation process is evolving. This book is based on first-hand experience of implementation of the complex bus system. And the many issues raised in this book would warrant newer analysis in emerging situations. We hope this book will be a forerunner for future research.

I.P. Gautam
H.M. Shivanand Swamy

Acknowledgements

The Government of Gujarat had decided to celebrate the calendar year 2005 as an Urban Year with an overall development agenda for urban Gujarat and the birth of Janmarg as an idea was conceived and given shape in the urban year as part of an integrated transit strategy for Ahmedabad city. The Gujarat Infrastructure Development Board, chaired by the Chief Minister Gujarat, had assigned the task of making a detailed project report for Ahmedabad city to CEPT University, and as decided by the State Government a DPR was approved and submitted to the Ministry of Urban Development, Government of India for further approval under JNNURM. After approval of the Project, Ahmedabad Municipal Corporation had incorporated an SPV: Ahmedabad Janmarg Limited: for speedy implementation and operation of the BRT System in Ahmedabad. The authors of this publication, who also worked on the project in different capacities would like to express gratitude to the State Government and then Honourable Chief Minister of Gujarat Shri Narendra Modi, Urban Development Ministers Shri Nitinbhai Patel and Smt. Anandiben Patel for the opportunity and their guidance.

This study and faster implementation was not possible without the active support of former Mayors of Ahmedabad, Shri Amitbhai Shah, Shri Kanajibhai Thakore, Shri Asit Vora, (both as standing Committee Chairman and subsequently as the Mayor) and Smt. Meenakshiben Patel. We are also grateful to all former Standing Committee Chairman, Smt. Madhuben Patel, Shri Bhupendrabhai Patel, Shri Pravinbhai Patel and also to the Chairman of AMTS including a team of Deputy Municipal Commissioners of AMC for their wholehearted support to the BRTS project and also ensuring smooth interface with citizens/stakeholders.

We would particularly like to acknowledge the support received from Shri Anil Baijal, Dr. M. Ramachandran, Dr. Sudhir Krishna former Secretaries of Ministry of Urban Development, and concerned Joint

Secretary Dr. O.P. Agarwal, Dr. S.K. Lohia for their active support and guidance from the Ministry. We are grateful to Smt. Manjula Subramaniam, then Chief Secretary Gujarat, and Additional Chief Secretaries Shri Kailashnathan, Shri S.R. Rao, Shri Paneervel, Smt. Gauri Kumar, Shri G.R. Aloria and concerned officials of State Government including Shri Anil Mukim, Shri C.L Meena, Shri A.K. Sharma, Shri K. Srinivas, Shri Jayant Parimal, Smt. D. Thara and We are also grateful to Dr. R.N. Vakil Director CEPT University, who have contributed significantly to the project at various times in the project cycle. We owe a special thanks to Dr. G.P. Mohapatra, former Municipal Commissioner and CMD, Ahmedabad Janmarg Limited who discussed with us the many dimensions of this work but is no longer with us to see this book.

We take this opportunity to gratefully acknowledge CEPT University through which the doctoral thesis "Development of Ahmedabad Bus Transit System: A Study of Innovations Using Actor-Network Theory" was completed by the first author. At the outset, we express our grateful thanks to Professor R. Parthasarathy for his continuous support and guidance. We would like to thank Dr. C.N. Ray and Prof. K.B. Jain, Dr. Bimal Patel of CEPT University and Dr. P.K. Sikdar former Professor of IIT for their valuable inputs during the course of the study.

We would also like to acknowledge the useful suggestions received from the dissertation examiners Dr David Webb (Newcastle University, UK), Dr. Sanjay Gupta (School of Planning & Architecture, Delhi) and Dr Saket Saraf (CEPT University, Ahmedabad), which went a long way in improving the overall quality of analysis.

This study would not have been possible without the help of the CEPT team (Centre of Excellence in Urban Transport) involved in designing BRTS Ahmedabad. Special thanks to Professor Dr. Shalini Sinha, Dr. Abhijit Lokre, Dr. Nitika Bhakuni, Mr. Amit Gotecha, Mr. Chintan Daftardar, Mr. Khelan Modi, Mr. Gautam Patel and Mr. Vijay Arya.

We also gratefully acknowledge the interest shown by Concept Publishing Company Pvt. Ltd. and thank them for bringing out this book.

I.P. Gautam
H.M. Shivanand Swamy

Contents

Abbreviations

AJL	:	Ahmedabad Janmarg Limited
AMC	:	Ahmedabad Municipal Corporation
AMTS	:	Ahmedabad Municipal Transport Service
ANT	:	Actor Network Theory
BRT	:	Bus Rapid Transit
BRTS	:	Bus Rapid Transit System
CAGR	:	Compound Annual Growth Rate
CEO	:	Chief Executive Officer
CEPT	:	Centre for Environmental Planning and Technology
CNG	:	Compressed Natural Gas
CO	:	Carbon Monoxide
CO_2	:	Carbon Dioxide
CPCB	:	Central Pollution Control Board
CRDF	:	Centre of Research and Development Foundation
DPR	:	Detailed Project Report
EoI	:	Expression of Interest
ETB	:	Electric Trolley Bus
GCC	:	Gross Cost Contract
GIDB	:	Gujarat Infrastructure Development Board
GoG	:	Government of Gujarat
GoI	:	Government of India
GVW	:	Gross Vehicle Weight
HCBS	:	High Capacity Bus System
HP	:	Horse Power
IC	:	Internal Combustion
ICE	:	Internal Combustion Engine
IIT	:	Indian Institute of Technology
INR	:	Indian Rs.
IRS	:	Indian Road Congress

ITMS	:	Intelligent Transportation Management System
ITS	:	Intelligent Transport System
JnNURM	:	Jawaharlal Nehru National Urban Reform Mission
LRT	:	Light Rapid Transit
MEGA	:	Metro-Link Express for Gandhinagar and Ahmedabad
MoUD	:	Ministry of Urban Development
MRT	:	Mass Rapid Transit
MRTS	:	Mass Rapid Transit Systems
Nox	:	Nitrogen Oxide
NUTP	:	National Urban Transport Policy
OPP	:	Obligatory Passage Point
PM	:	Particulate Matter
PMT	:	Private Motorised Transport
ROB	:	Rail Over Bridge
RF	:	Radio Frequency
RFID	:	Radio Frequency Identification
RfP	:	Request for Proposal
RITES	:	Rail India Techno Economic Services
RoW	:	Right of Way
RSP	:	Respiratory Suspended Particulate
SHS	:	State Highway System
SMC	:	Surat Municipal Corporation
SPM	:	Suspended Particulate Matter
UAs	:	Urban Agglomerations
UDD	:	Urban Development Department
ULSD	:	Ultra Low Sulphur Diesel
V/C	:	Volume/Capacity

List of Figures and Tables

FIGURES

TABLES

1
Introduction
Understanding Development of Large Infrastructure Projects

1.1 Introduction

The forward march of economic growth and technology has resulted in the evolution of faster and more flexible modes of transportation through the ages. "The usual trajectory is from human or animal powered forms of transportation — such as walking, bicycle or ox carts — to motorised public transportation — in the form of the bus or minibus — and finally to motorised private transportation — usually in the form of the automobile" (Dapice, Gomez-Ibanez & Thanh, 2010: 9). In turn, innovations and developments in mobility systems have shaped our cities in a significant way.

Sustainability and efficiency goals have necessitated stemming the overbearing reliance of cities on private transport and instead redirecting efforts towards the strengthening of public transport. Metro rail and rail-based transport modes have been popular in the West but due to affordability issues their appeal has been limited in the context of the cities of the developing world. This where the Bus Rapid Transport System (BRTS) assumes importance since it promises a "high-quality bus based transit system that delivers fast, comfortable, and cost effective urban mobility through the provision of segregated right-of-way infrastructure, rapid and frequent operations, and excellence in marketing and customer service" (The Bus Rapid Transit Planning Guide, 2007).

The BRTS delivers fast and efficient mobility at a fraction of the cost of say the Metro Rail. Curitiba in Brazil is considered the pioneering city that innovated on the concept while Bogota in Columbia is hailed for developing a system that rivals the rail in terms of sheer capacity. Following these fine examples, many more cities in the world especially those from the Global South, including several Indian cities, have since then attempted to develop a BRTS tailor-made for their own requirements. The research on which this book is based is framed in this context of the developing world as a pioneer in a segment of urban planning, occupied by public transport innovation rather than being a stereotypical passive adopter.

1.2 Urban Transport in India

India is fast transforming into an urban society. As per the 2011 Census, 377 million people accounting for 31 per cent of the country's population were living in urban areas. Estimates suggest that by 2031, the urban population will reach 600 million, and the urbanisation rate will rise from 31 per cent to 40 per cent (Rogers & Shoemaker, 1971). Though new towns will emerge, large cities will continue to remain attractive and experience rapid growth. The number of large cities is also expected to rise. In 2011 there were 50 cities with a million-plus population; these are likely to increase to 87 by 2031 (Swamy & Sinha, 2014).

Studies suggest that large cities have a relative advantage in terms of wealth creation and concentration (Bettencourt, Lobo, & Strumsky, 2007) (Pratham, 2014). Transport plays a central role in the life of large cities. Large cities have seen a rapid pace of motorisation and increased use of private vehicles, as evidenced by a decline in the share of buses (from 11.1 per cent in 1951 to 1.1 per cent in 2011 to 0.69 per cent in 2019), when compared to all registered vehicles (MoRTH, 2019)[1]. The increase in private vehicle share is attributed to the decline and deficiencies in the country's existing public transport system. "Extreme congestion, long commute times, choking air pollution, deadly traffic accidents, and inadequate public transport are the norm. Billions of dollars in economic productivity are lost due to congestion. Air and noise pollution severely impact health and quality of life. The poor lack affordable or comfortable mobility" (Taiyab, 2008: 1).

Efforts to develop public transportation systems in Indian cities have been underway for some time now. Until 2006, these efforts mainly focused on developing rail-based mass rapid transit systems

(MRTS). Rail India Techno Economic Services (RITES) prepared feasibility reports for several large cities. Indian Railways initiated building India's first metro rail system in Kolkata in 1972. The system, covering a length of 27.22 km was opened for commercial services in 1984, after a long delay. Today, it carries approximately 650,000 passengers daily. In Delhi, metro rail system planning began in 1984 and construction in 1998, with the system opening for commercial services in 2002.[2] Though metro rail systems have been attractive and many cities aspire to develop them, it is argued that "there is a need to consider lower cost alternatives, for example, bus-based systems..." due to the high capital and operating costs and the length of time taken from conception to commercial operations of metro systems (Mohan, NA).

The Ministry of Urban Development, Government of India initiated the drafting of the National Urban Transport Policy (NUTP) in 2004 and adopted it in 2006. NUTP argued for a shift in focus from vehicle movements to the mobility of people and goods, suggesting 'equitable allocation of road space' as a principal strategy. Along with the adoption of NUTP, the Ministry of Urban Development also announced a reform-linked urban investment programme, JnNURM, in 2005. The scope of the programme covered funding support for urban transportation, including roads, highways, expressways, MRTS and metro projects (Jnnurm.nic, 2015). An international conference on alternative mass transit systems was organised by the Ministry in 2005, in which Bus Rapid Transit Systems (BRTS) emerged as a serious option for Indian cities. The first set of BRTS proposals from three cities were approved under JnNURM in 2006. It appeared that BRTS innovation was being successfully transferred to the Indian subcontinent.

Three cities — Pune, Delhi, and Ahmedabad — took the lead with initiating the BRTS proposals. Of them, Ahmedabad was well ahead with the preparation of its Detailed Project Report (DPR) for planning BRTS when the JnNURM programme was announced. The city submitted its DPR for support under JnNURM in 2006. The first phase of BRTS DPR, for a proposed 58 km corridor, was approved by the Ministry of Urban Development in 2006 in two stages, on August 11, 2006, and October 6, 2006. The second phase (of 30 km) was approved on August 19, 2008. A total network of 88 km was thus approved for Ahmedabad under JnNURM.[3]As on March 2021, Ahmedabad's operational BRT network is 97 km. Additionally, MRTS network is being developed for 72.5 km.

In Delhi, on the other hand, BRTS (formally referred to as High Capacity Bus System or HCBS) was fully funded by the Delhi State Government and was developed for a stretch of 5.8 km. The focus of the project was mainly on the development of a pilot corridor, which was made operational in 2007. For a variety of reasons, the system did not receive the expected support from opinion-makers and the media (Singh, 2012). Hence, the Delhi Government was unable to expand beyond the initial 5.8 km stretch. This limiting of the operational stretch perhaps prevented HCBS from achieving its true potential, and the corridor was dismantled by the Delhi Government in 2015.

In addition to Ahmedabad, two other cities, Indore and Pune, also submitted detailed project reports for building a BRTS under JnNURM funding, by recasting their earlier road development proposals. Along with Ahmedabad, they were the first to receive JnNURM funding for a pilot corridor length (of about 12 km each) in 2006. Subsequently, eight other cities availed JnNURM funding for implementing a BRT system. In addition, two other cities — Naya Raipur and Hubli-Dharwad — initiated BRT projects supported by the Ministry of Urban Development, Government of India under the Sustainable Urban Transport Project of the Government of India and the World Bank. Table 1.1 presented have shows the status of BRT systems in cities in India.

As may be deciphered from Table 1.1, the initial enthusiasm for the adoption of BRTS was not sustained. By March 2019, India had only 10 functional BRT systems, accounting for 328 km of operational corridor length. The city of Ahmedabad has successfully expanded the network. The other systems functioning well are Surat, Hubli-Dharwad and Indore, which again are modelled on the Ahmedabad BRTS. After 15 years of national government support to cities for building BRTS, only the Ahmedabad BRTS and three others developed on the Ahmedabad model, appear to have caught the imagination of the people and have been recognised as successful systems, by the citizens and the governments as well as by national and international agencies. This leads us to a series of questions related to project development.

Is Ahmedabad BRTS a success? If so, how did Ahmedabad successfully conceptualise, develop and implement it? Generalising

Table 1.1: Status of BRT Systems in Cities in India

Sl. No.	BRT Cities	Population in Million (2011)*	Funding From	Year of Sanctioning of Funding**	Network Length Sanctioned in km**	Network Length Operational in km	Status	Date of Start of Operations
1.	Delhi	11.4	State Government	2004		5.8	Dismantled in 2016	April 2008
2.	Ahmedabad	5.6	JnNURM Government of India	August 2006, October 2006, August 2008	88.5	97 (88.5+8.5 shared)	Operational	October 2009
3.	Jaipur	3.1	JnNURM Government of India	July 2007, January 2009	39.45	20	Operational – Partial	July 2010
4.	Rajkot	1.3	JnNURM Government of India	July 2007	29	10.7	Operational	January 2012
5.	Bhopal	1.8	JnNURM Government of India	November 2006	42.2	24	Operational	September 2013
6.	Indore	1.9	JnNURM Government of India	August 2006, September 2013	11.65	11.4	Operational	December 2013

(Contd.)

Sl. No.	BRT Cities	Population in Million (2011)*	Funding From	Year of Sanctioning of Funding**	Network Length Sanctioned in km**	Network Length Operational in km	Status	Date of Start of Operations
7.	Surat	4.5	JnNURM Government of India	March 2008	29.9	101 (29.9+71.1 SMC funding)	Operational	January 2014
8.	Pune-Pimpri Chinchwad	3.1	JnNURM Government of India	August 2006, October 2006, March 2007, December 2007, August 2008, November 2008	157	22.5	Operational — Partial	August 2015
9.	Amritsar	1.1	JnNURM Government of India	January 2014	31	9	Operational — Partial	December 2016
10	Vijayawada	1.05	JnNURM Government of India	March 2007	15.2	10	Operational — Partial	2013
11	Vishakhapatnam	1.7	JnNURM Government of India	March 2007	45.2		Under Implementation	
12	Kolkata	14.1	JnNURM Government of India	June 2010	15.5		Under Implementation	

(Contd.)

Sl. No.	BRT Cities	Population in Million (2011)*	Funding From	Year of Sanctioning of Funding**	Network Length Sanctioned in km**	Network Length Operational in km	Status	Date of Start of Operations
13	Naya Raipur	NA	The World Bank, SUTP Project of the GoI	NA	56		Under Implementation	
14	Hubli Dharwad	0.9	The World Bank, SUTP Project of the GoI	NA	22.4	22.4	Operational	October 2018

Source: Sinha, 2019.

this to large infrastructure projects, the key questions that emerge are:

- How is the success or failure of large infrastructure projects measured?
- How are such large infrastructure projects conceptualised, developed and implemented?

This publication attempts to explain responses to these by adopting the Actor-Network Theory, using the Ahmedabad BRTS as a case.

1.3 Approaches to understand large scale Infrastructure Project Development Processes

There are alternative approaches to understand project development process.

1.3.1 Traditional Approaches

The first, a project management approach based on rational decision-making processes which adopts the triangle of objectives: time, cost and quality.[4] The project is classified as a success or failure based on the performance against these three objectives. Improvisations to this approach have been suggested by modifying or adding criteria dealing with project objectives and outcomes (Kliem and Ludin, 1992, Nelson, 2005).

By adopting pre-defined factors such as proper planning, a clear statement of requirements, realistic expectation, availability and adequacy of resources, user involvement, executive management support etc., based on stakeholders' perception, key elements influencing the success of the projects are identified.

The diffusion of innovation theory by Rogers (2003) attempts to model the rate of diffusion of a new idea from its conception to final adoption. Whether diffusion takes place or not, and its rate, is considered measures of success, and the inherent characteristics of the technology are regarded as key drivers of success.

An important study addressing the success or failure of 30 mega transport projects that have adopted financial, policy and durability criteria as measures of success, and have identified the procurement and financing as key to the project success is of Roger *et al.* (2008). Dimitrious *et al.* (2014) highlighted the shortcomings of relying on project management criteria of finishing projects on time, within budget, and according to specification and emphasised the importance of 'emergent objectives' in appraising project achievements. Critical success factors identified were the treatment of risk, uncertainty and complexity in mega transport project decision-making, with special attention paid to the impact of changing contexts on such decision-making (Dimitrious *et al.*, 2014).

These approaches more commonly known as the traditional view of project development are based on the following three premises:

(i) Tendency to assume success or failure as an 'end state,' and that the factors could be isolated as causes which affect the success of projects.
(ii) Assuming that project development is a linear process of planning, design, and implementation. There are eight distinct phases in a design process: definition of the problem, formulation of objectives, conceptual design, the definition of alternatives, and selection of the best alternative, detailed design, construction, and operation (Dym, 1994).
(iii) The role of the project designer is assumed to be critical in deciding the fate of the project.

These approaches are "perfectly appropriate when the project is to construct and commission some physical entity involving known technologies in a stable organizational context. In this context, one in which the specification of the project is, at least in the outline form, complete and known before undertaking it, the idea of decomposing the project task through techniques of 'work breakdown' and through 'organisational breakdown', then aligning the two in work package design is entirely reasonable" (Alderman, Ivory, McLoughlin, and Vaughan, 2014: 5). Therefore, the adoption of this approach to project development is appropriate when the technology is known to users and planners equally, and when a previously established system is merely being prototyped.

1.3.2 Alternate Approaches

BRTS and such other large infrastructure projects are enormous and complex public projects, and designing and developing these means inserting them into an existing urban arena, replacing the existing. The conflicts are evident with several already established interests making such inserts difficult. Traditional approaches to understand these would only provide a partial explanation. An alternate perspective drawn from the Actor-Network Theory (ANT) is proposed in this book.

This argues that "... success or failure is a product of the alliances that are mobilised, rather than the inherent qualities that are possessed" (Scott-Smith, 2013: 1). ANT suggests that success and failure are social accomplishments of many different human and non-human actors that lie in the hands of those who come after the innovation's 'inventor' (Latour, 1987: 259). Further, studies show that such sequential processes are the exception rather than the norm (Andreasen & Jensen, 2010: 7). Also, case studies and empirical analyses show that the overlapping in time and the overlapping in distribution among teams and persons of tasks that analytically belong to different phases blur these sequenced phases if they exist at all (Ardila & Gomez, 2004) as cited in Felipe & Pineda, 2010: 12). In such non-linear processes of innovation project development, "Latour suggests that the success/failure of a machine or technology cannot be predicted with a list of social factors" (Briers & Chua, 2011: 240). Unlike the traditional approach, ANT views success or failure as a dynamic status.

Application of ANT in the understanding of infrastructure development throws up three broad perspectives: the first relates to understanding the design and development of infrastructure projects as actor-networks; the second is the co-evolutionary perspectives wherein the transportation system and the city evolve together, analysed using the concept of arenas of development and the politics of urban mobility; and the third attempts to analyse the shifts in policy focus from that of transportation to that of sustainable mobility.

Adopting the concepts of Actor-Network Theory, Translation, Black-Box and Distribution of Agency, an attempt is made to understand the development of large and complex public sector infrastructure projects. In the process, an attempt is made to highlight the shifts occurring in the urban transportation focus towards sustainable mobility.

The Concept of Translation

Tom Scott-Smith (2013) in his paper rejecting the common view that projects succeed based on their superior objectives, planning and implementation, proposes an alternative perspective drawn from Actor-Network Theory: that success or failure is a product of the alliances that are mobilised, rather than the inherent qualities that are possessed. This argument is illustrated regarding a 1970s development project, which involved the extraction of protein from plant leaves to provide a nutritional supplement for diets in Nigeria. By drawing on archival sources, the paper reconstructs the main actors involved in the project, analyses what caused them to become involved, and then turns attention to how these alliances fell apart. It uses three concepts of ANT: the idea of 'black boxes,' the concept of translation, and the involvement of material objects which provide durability to actor-networks. Examining the development projects as actor-networks, which rely on mobilising allies in order to succeed, it is argued that the larger and more influential development projects are the ones that have managed to mobilise more extensive and durable alliances, and the less successful development projects are built on restricted and weaker alliances. This is a deviation from the prevailing view amongst development practitioners that success can be explained by the project's inherent qualities and measured against stated aims and objectives.

Innovation studies tend to focus on the 'new technology' while ignoring the resistance from the existing ones that are being displaced. Inadequate attention paid to the 'existing' may prove fatal to the innovation. Ahmedabad successfully introduced BRTS while maintaining a focus on the 'existing' in the city of Ahmedabad. This chapter presents the efforts of the focal actors to convert the competition to a collaborative effort of the existing regular bus system operated by the Ahmedabad Municipal Transport System (AMTS), a potential metro rail system, and the informal public transport system delivered through auto-rickshaws.

An attempt has been made to illustrate how BRTS was selected, conceptualised and developed successfully through the mobilisation of alliances of actors in the development arena, turning potential competitors into collaborators.

Black Boxes — Artifacts, Programme of Action, Scripts and Inscriptions

The project was built on three black boxes: the first — a scientific fact is that the protein gap and the extraction of leaf protein concentrate as a cheap source of protein; the second that the important stakeholders— the community of experts, the donor agency, the beneficiaries, the leaves and the machinery — had agreed with the project interest; and the non-human allies — the leaves and curd, mills and vats, knives and hoes, and the packet of leaf protein concentrates with logos and designs — were able to provide more durable form. Despite over a decade of effort with large sums of money spent, the project still fell apart in the 1980s. As noted by the researcher, "nothing revolutionary occurred that caused the failure of the project, but there was, instead, a gradual dissolution of alliances that held the whole idea together" (Tom Scott-Smith, 2013). This was due to poor translation in the beginning which led to the gradual dissolution of the association with time.

Bruno Latour explored how artifacts can be deliberately designed to both replace human action and constrain and shape the actions of other humans (Latour, 2015: 2). His study demonstrated how people can 'act at a distance' through the technologies they create and implement, and how, from a user's perspective, technology can appear to determine or compel certain actions. He argued that even technologies that are so commonplace that we do not even think about them can shape the decisions we make, the effects our actions have, and the way we move through the world. Technologies play such an important role in mediating human relationships, Latour argued, that we cannot understand how societies work without an understanding of how technologies shape our everyday lives. Latour's study of the relationship between producers, machines and users demonstrates how certain values and political goals can be achieved through the construction and employment of technologies.

An attempt is made to showcase how the Ahmedabad BRTS designers deliberately designed certain artifacts to ensure exclusivity.

Distribution of Agency

Valderrama and Jorgensen (2008) explored the socio-technical dynamics of developing new urban transport systems adopting two concepts of ANT: Distribution of Agency and Arenas of Development, built on Actor-Network Theory, taking Transmilenio in Bogotá and the Metro in Copenhagen as case studies. ANT attributes agency to both humans and non-humans; as part of the design process, *actants* who are part of the network would negotiate and actively distribute agency in the new system. The study on the Transmilenio case traces how designers, investors and politicians decided on a high platform, integrated bus system.

Valderrama and Jorgensen (2008) conceived the city as an arena of development defined by various pre-existing transport technologies, institutions, activities that have evolved over a period, layer by layer. The concept of an arena of development is used to account for relations between new and pre-existing actor-networks and to explain how the transportation system and the city emerge in this co-evolutionary process. The paper illustrated that when spaces of a city are reconstructed, or new transport infrastructures added, changes occur not only within the new spaces or systems but in the city at large, by reconfiguring relations and providing possibilities for new ways of perceiving and making sense of the city.

Analysing transportation infrastructure investments towards the production of BRT Lines, urban highways and toll roads, a bike-share programme and bike lines, by the former Mexico City Mayor Marcelo Ebrard' during his six years in office, Lopez (2013) attempts to illustrate the "ongoing transformation in the way transportation policy is conceived: a sort of paradigm shift from transportation policy to urban mobility policy." Further, the author argues that the shift to urban mobility policy introduces "different dimensions and qualitative objectives and requirements for transportation policy, including sustainability, equity and citizen participation."

Even though urban mobility is a concept which does not have a legal or normative framework (which is also true in India), the author attempts to illustrate how urban mobility is used as a way of transforming the city as a 'more democratic city,' making the planning process more inclusive by introducing 'mandatory citizen input and participation' aimed at making planning projects production of 'services that truly respond to user's needs' and 'not disproportionately affecting poor and disadvantaged citizens.' This brings about new alliances between state and non-state actors bringing about new synergies and conflicts as well.

The design of urban transport systems is a process where the actors involved negotiate and actively distribute agency among the components of the new system. How the agency is distributed among the actants is crucial to the stabilisation of new transport systems. In the ANT approach, a basic assumption is that of 'non-determinism, whereby neither human actions nor technologies are assumed to exert direct causal impacts. Rather, consequences are seen to result from the interplay of competing infrastructures, conflicting objectives, the preferences of different social groups, and chance' (Markus & Robey, 1988 as cited in Rhodes, J., 2009: 4).

Buses are the most critical element influencing the performance as well as the attractiveness of the system, and in Ahmedabad, their selection involved multiple stakeholders whose interests were diverse. Some of the concerns related to the choice of vehicles were vehicle design, fuel choice and operating mode.

1.4 Chapter Scheme

There are six chapters in this book. This introductory chapter has sought to introduce the context and the alternate approaches to understand large urban infrastructure projects.

The second chapter presents the concept of BRTS and traces its evolution in various cities of the world.

The third chapter looks at the Actor-Network Theory with special emphasis on the appropriateness of the innovation translation concept as a method to analyse the design and development of complex technological projects such as the BRTS.

The fourth chapter foregrounds how focal actors in Ahmedabad introduced the BRTS in the city while keeping the focus on the 'existing' in the city thereby converting the competition into a collaborative effort comprising the AMTS bus service, a potential metro rail system, and the informal PT system offered by the auto-rickshaws and the new innovation of the BRTS.

The fifth chapter, adopting the concept of black-box (artifacts, devices, scripts and inscriptions), attempts to explain how non-humans are designed to influence human behaviour.

In chapter six, how various regulatory, technical, organisational and human actors act together to negotiate decisions are detailed. The decisions in such a system emerge from an interactive process between networks of actors with different viewpoints.

The last chapter is the concluding and summarising one.

NOTES

1. The total number of registered motor vehicles in India increased from about 0.3 million (as on March 1951) to about 142 million (as on 31 March, 2011) to about 296 million (as on March 2019). The total registered vehicles in the country grew at a CAGR of 9.9 per cent between 2001 and 2011(Ministry of Road Transport and Highways, 2012).
2. Subsequently metro rail system has expanded at a fast pace and is now spread over 200 km and carrying an average of 2.5 million passengers daily (Delhi Metro Rail Co., 2016: 9).
3. As per JnNURM, for cities/UAs with 4 million plus population going by the 2001 Census, grant amount from the Central Government was 35 per cent, while from the State Government it was 15 per cent, with the balance to be borne by the local authority (GoI, 2005).
4. The triangle of objectives is attributed to the work of Barnes (1980). He subsequently replaced the criteria 'quality' by 'performance.' Quality implies conforming to specifications, whereas performance implies that the project 'does what it is supposed to do.'

2
Actor Network Theory
An Overview

2.1 Introduction

Schumpeter (1939) argues that innovation is the key to success for private businesses. It helps them to cut costs, improve product quality and opens up new markets, thereby helping them to remain competitive and profitable. Failure to innovate would mean that a private business would have to shut operations sooner rather than later. According to Sorensen and Torfing, the situation in the public sector is not different. Many people, and especially a good deal of those employed in the private sector, consider the public sector as a slow-moving bureaucracy characterised by red tape, inertia and stalemate (Sorensen & Torfing, 2012: 2). However, there are observable changes in public sector operations which have a significant impact on service delivery. In fact, most large-scale innovations are undertaken either by the public sector directly, or through its (funding) support, including that to the public sector itself (OECD, 2014).

Besides reviewing the concepts of ANT, this chapter attempts to evolve an analytical framework based on the empirical studies carried out.

2.2 Defining Innovation

The concept of innovation has been defined in different ways. The Oxford Dictionary defines 'to innovate' as 'making changes in something established, especially by introducing new methods, ideas, or products.' According to Schumpeter, '*innovation* (*only*) pertains to a commercially exploitable novelty' (as cited in Moldaschl, 2010: 2). Further, Schumpeter argues that innovation 'combines factors in a new way, or ... consists in carrying out new combinations' (Schumpeter, 1939: 84).

Rogers defines 'innovation' as 'an idea, practice, or project that is perceived as new by an individual or other unit of adoption' (Rogers E., 2003: 12), while Albury states that "[s]uccessful innovation is the creation and implementation of new processes, products, services and methods of delivery which result in significant improvements in outcomes, efficiency, effectiveness or quality" (Albury, 2005). Others define innovation as something that does not have to be entirely new, but is 'at least a significant departure from the conventional practice in a field' (Moore, 2005: 45). Hartely (2006) states that innovation is 'the successful development, implementation and use of new or structurally improved products, processes, services or organisational forms' (as cited in Mastic, 2012: 4).

Schumpeter (1939) described development as a historical process of structural changes, substantially driven by innovations. He categorised innovation into five types:

(i) introduction of a new good that is one with which consumers are not yet familiar, or of a new quality of a good,
(ii) introduction of a new method of production, which need not be founded upon a new scientific discovery, and can also exist in a new way of handling a commodity commercially,
(iii) opening of a new market into which the particular branch of manufacture of the country in question has not previously entered, whether or not this market has existed before,
(iv) conquest of a new source of supply of raw materials or half-manufactured goods, again irrespective of whether this source already exists or whether it has first to be created, and
(v) carrying out of the new organisation of any industry, as in the creation of a monopoly position (for example, through trustification) or the breaking up of a monopoly position.

Irrespective of the type of innovation, it is also important to understand whether the organisation is engaged in the production of goods or services. Service innovation can be an amalgamation of product innovation, that is, 'the introduction of a new product, or a significant qualitative change in an existing product,' and process innovation, that is, 'the introduction of a new process for making or delivering goods and services' (Greenhalgh & Rogers, 2007: 4). Den Hertog defines innovation in services as an interplay of service concepts, service delivery systems, client interfaces, and technologies (Hertog, 2000: 21) that often entails new ways in which customers view and use the service (Agarwal, R., 2011: 1172). It may include a new service concept, a new client interface, a new service delivery system or new technological options. It may even be a combination of all of these. At least two peculiarities — the intangibility of services, and their simultaneous production and consumption — distinguish a service from a product, and have a bearing on the concept of service innovation.

The OECD defines public-sector innovation 'as the implementation by a public-sector organisation of new or significantly improved operations or products' (OECD, 2014). To put it simply, public sector innovation involves creating, developing and implementing practical ideas that achieve a public benefit. These ideas have to be at least in part new (rather than improvements); they have to be taken up and used (rather than simply remaining ideas); and they have to be useful. By this definition, innovation overlaps with, but is different from, creativity and entrepreneurship (Mulgan, 2014: 5). Public sector innovation may refer to significant improvements to public administration and/or services. Innovation may apply to the structure of the public sector itself, or the way in which public services are provided. The OECD further identified a number of forms by which innovation may take place within the public sector, at the service level or the policy level (OECD, 2014).

2.3 Actor-Network Theory

Actor-Network Theory (ANT), developed in the 1980s by sociologists Bruno Latour, Michel Callon and John Law, has its origins in the field of the study of science and technology. ANT is also known as 'Enrolment Theory,' the 'Sociology of Translation' or the 'Sociology of Association.' It provides a framework for investigating society, science and technology, and explains the process of the construction and maintenance of networks. ANT acts as a toolkit to explore how human and non-human actors interact with one another to make sense of their world (Latour, 2005).

The vocabulary of ANT is presented in Table 2.1.

2.3.1 *Actor-Network Theory: Vocabulary and Definitions*

ANT is difficult to summarise as it has a very large number of concepts. Over the years, researchers have developed a unique vocabulary, which is presented in Table 2.1.

Table 2.1: ANT Vocabulary and Concepts

Concept	Explanation
Methodological Principles • Generalised agnosticism • Generalised symmetry Free association	Callon 1986: 3) defines three principles of translation. This means that "there is no point of view which is privileged and no interpretation is censored." Impartial analysis is granted to actors, whether they are human or non-human. Symmetry according to ANT means that there is no fixed identity for actors. The identity and the importance of any actor is always negotiated through network interactions. ANT does not distinguish between natural and social phenomena. These distinctions are the effects of networked activity, are not causal, and cannot provide explanations.
Actor/Actant	'Any element which bends space around itself, makes other elements dependent upon itself and translates their will into the language of its own' (Latour & Callon, 1981: 286).
Intermediary	'An intermediary, in my vocabulary, is what transports meaning or force without transformation: defining its inputs is enough to define its outputs' (Latour, 2005: 39).
Mediator	An active presence between actors, 'mediators transform, translate, distort, and modify the meaning of the elements they are supposed to carry' (Latour, 2005: 39).
Actor-Network	'A heterogeneous network of aligned interests formed through translation of interests' (Walsham & Sahay, 1999: 42).
Assemblages	Built out of social ties rather than physical, and explores what the social is made of, e.g. how we act, or who else is acting (Carroll, N., 2014: 125).
Associations	Non-social ties which can be used to trace associations and do not designate a thing among other things (Carroll, N., 2014: 125).

(Contd.)

Concept	Explanation
Black Box	A snapshot of the network which illustrates its irreversible properties (Carroll, N., 2014: 125). Successful actor-networks construct themselves on these black boxes, which are essentially just other actor-networks that have reached a high degree of stability in their own right.
Translation 1. Problematisation 2. Interessement 3. Enrolment 4. Mobilisation	The creation process of an actor-network through four main phases (Callon, Some Elements of a Sociology of Translation: Domestication of the Scallops and the Fishermen of St. Brieuc Bay, 1986: 196). 1. How to become indispensable. Defines identities and interests of other actors which align with its own interests (i.e. obligatory passage point). 2. How the allies are locked into place (convince other actors to agree on and accept the definition of the focal actor). 3. How to define and coordinate roles. (An actor accepts the interests defined by the focal actor and sets out to achieve them through actant allies, which align with the actor-network). 4. Mobilisation of allies. Ensuring that actors represent their interests.
Obligatory Passage Point (OPP)	A situation that has to occur in order for all the actors to satisfy their interests (Latour, 1992 as cited in Carroll, 2014: 125).
Inscription	Creating technical objects which ensure that an actor's interests are protected, e.g. a particular piece of software or regulations to meet organisational objectives (Latour, 1992) as cited in (Carroll, 2014: 125).
Irreversibility	The point to which it is impossible to return; a point where alterative opportunities may exist (Walsham & Sahay, 1999: 42)
Speaker/delegate/ representative	An actor who speaks on behalf of (or stands in for) others (Callon, M., 1986, as cited in Carroll, 2014: 125).
Betrayal	A situation where actors do not abide by the agreements arising from the enrolment of their representatives (Latour, 1992, as cited in Carroll, 2014: 125).

Source: Adapted from Carroll, 2014.

Actors in *ANT,* as presented in the table above, are those who 'act' to pursue other actors to align their interests with their own. The actors may be human or non-human, individual or collective, material or immaterial. Callon defines an actor as 'any entity able to associate texts, humans, non-humans and money' (Callon, 1991: 140). They are also termed as actants or agents, and can associate or disassociate freely with other actants.

"Actants enter into networked associations, which in turn define them, name them, and provide them with substance, action, intention, and subjectivity" (Ritzer, 2005: 1). It is important to note that activity is granted to an actor "by another ... an actant can literally be anything provided it is granted to be the source of action" (Latour & Callon, 1981: 286).

2.3.2 *Three Main Concepts of ANT*

The focus of the present book is on presenting the theory and practice of setting up of large-scale urban transport projects, taking the Ahmedabad Bus Rapid Transit System as a case. Three main concepts of ANT: translation, inscription, and distribution of agency are used to explain the practice of developing large-scale transport projects.

2.3.2.1 *Translation*

The process of the creation and maintenance of actor-networks is termed translation. In other words, translation is the process of converting entities, of making them similar (such that one entity may be substituted for another), or of simplifying (black-boxing or translating network elements into a single block) while retaining difference (translation is not simply transfer). According to Callon (1986: 3), the translation process consists of four major moments: problematisation, interessement, enrolment and mobilisation of allies. Using the case of scallop harvesting in the 1970s in St. Brieuc Bay, France (presented in the box below), Callon illustrates these concepts as:

Problematisation

At this stage, the primary actors analyse a situation, define the problem and propose a solution to deal with it, thereby rendering themselves indispensable. The problems are defined such that others can also recognise them as their problem and participate in resolving them. By being part of this process, the primary actors make themselves indispensable, and thereby establish an obligatory passage point (OPP).

The Device of 'Interessement' (Interposition), or How the Allies are Locked into Place

At the interessement stage, the primary actors seek to convince other actors to agree on and accept their definition of the focal actor (Callon, 1986). They attempt to recruit other relevant actors to assume roles in the network with a view to 'lock them into place.' During the interessement phase of a translation process, various devices can be used to strengthen the association between actors and to support the structure of the network (Latour, 1992).

Enrolment, or How to Define and Coordinate Roles

ANT is also called the Theory of Enrolment (Ritzer, 2005: 1). At the stage of enrolment, roles are defined and formally accepted by actors. To describe enrolment is thus to describe the group of multilateral negotiations, trials of strength and tricks that accompany interessement, and enable its success (Callon, 1986: 10). To succeed means that the solution is accepted as a new concept by the actors, and a new network of interests is generated. Enrolment is a process of negotiation that exhibits how interessement meets the actors' interests, and persuades them to accept the new actor-network (Carroll, Richardson, & Whelan, 2012).

Illustrative Case: Scallop harvesting in the 1970s in St. Brieuc Bay, France

The Problem: Over-harvesting of scallops in Brest, which led to a decline in their stocks in St. Brieuc Bay.

Callon, in his 1986 study, identified the relevant actors and their motives/interests. The process involved as primary actors three researchers who studied a sustainable Japanese practice of scallop harvesting called the Scallop Breeding Programme. This commercial technique of harvesting scallops involved anchoring larvae to sheltered collectors, and sowing immature larvae on the ocean bed to develop further. The other actors were the St. Brieuc Bay fishermen who looked for large profits; the scallops which had to save themselves from the predators; and the scientific community, which was interested in generating new knowledge about the scallops' sustainability. The scallop breeding programme's stability and unity of the alliance was subverted when the scallops and then the

(Contd.)

fishermen did not cooperate. This dissidence led to eventual dissolution of the actor network.

The problem was to identify a system of alliances between entities that must be constructed in order to achieve specific goals. The goals included: altering the interest of fishermen from short-term profits to long-term assured profits, scallops attempting to perpetuate themselves, the scientific community accepting new knowledge, and the researchers developing advanced knowledge so that scallops could be repopulated. The three researchers, through this redefinition of goals, became the obligatory passage point (OPP).

At the interessement stage, while the evincing of interest in the problemitisation was more or less straightforward, getting scallops to flourish was a challenge. An experiment of artificial construction was done towards interessement. Representatives of the fishermen discussed the reasons for the scallops' extinction. Collectors agreed to take up the role of protecting the larvae from predators. Lack of knowledge about scallops was discussed at scientific conferences and in scientific publications. Through this process the scallop breeding programme was acccpted as the way forward by the various actors.

Simply put, enrolment means 'getting the actors to act out their roles (i.e. to form the relevant alliances and associations)' (Callon, 1986). In case of the scallops breeding programme, the key challenge was how to get scallops to negotiate currents, parasites and different types of collection bags. The research experiment showed that scallops anchor only in certain conditions. The findings of the experiment were convincing and were accepted by other actors.

In case of the scallops breeding programme, the principal actors, namely the three researchers, became the legitimate representatives to speak on behalf of the wider scientific community, the fishermen, and the scallops.

However, the alliance formed was not stable as the scallops and the fishermen did not accept their roles. The dissidence and betrayal from the two ultimately led to the failure of the translation process.

The Mobilisation of Allies

Mobilisation, the final moment of translation, relates to a set of manners utilised by a focal actor to ensure that all actors have legitimate speakers to represent them in groups, and thus avoid betrayal (Callon, 1986).

Speakers or representatives are actors who speak or deputise for other actors (Walsham, 1997).

Mobilisation also means that the network is stabilised, i.e. negotiations in the network enable alignment of interests of the actors with those of the actor-network to a greater degree. Failure to mobilise, i.e. the betrayal of actors in the alignment of interests would result in a destabilised network. Here, the new network starts to operate in a target-oriented manner to implement the proposed solution (Callon, 1986).

In the formation of a network, multiple translation processes occur across time and space, which is termed as Chains of Translation (Latour, 1992). These 'refer to the work through which actors modify, displace, and translate their various and contradictory interests.' With each translation, the network evolves and grows.

2.3.2.2 *Artifacts, Programme of Action, Scripts and Inscriptions*

To *inscribe* means to build an actor-network. It means to inscribe a programme of action into technology and artifacts for the users. Actors have diverse interests that are continually negotiated within the network. To bring about stability in the network, primary actors (designers) work out a scenario of how the system will be used, and accordingly develop a programme of action for the users. The action programme thus evolved is then inscribed into artifacts, defining the pattern of use. This is the way that agency is delegated to non-human actants, which would then shape human behaviour and also make the network stable. Latour (1991) suggests that "whenever we discover a stable social relation, it is the introduction of some non-humans that accounts for this relative stability" (Latour, 1991: 111).

Illustrative Case: Hotel Key

The Problem: Hotel customers do not return their room keys when leaving the premises.

Latour (1991) provided an illustration of the concept of a programme of action and inscription using the example of the hotel key. To prevent loss, misplacement etc., hotels seek to ensure that guests leave keys at the front desk when leaving. Various means are used to establish this behaviour as expected: one is to put a sign behind the counter stating 'Please remember to return the key.' Often, people

(*Contd.*)

do not notice this sign or ignore it. A second is to have the doorman remind customers to leave behind their keys. In yet another attempt, hotels resorted to a non-human actor, by adding a large metal tag to the key. The heavy tag forced the customers to obey the programme of action. Through successive translations, a stable actor-network was established.

As put by Akrich, '[d]esigners thus define actors with specific tastes, competencies, motives, aspirations, political prejudices, and the rest, and they assume that morality, technology, science, and economy will evolve in particular ways. A large part of the work of innovators is that of "inscribing" this vision of (or prediction about) the world in the technical content of the new object. (...) The technical realisation of the innovator's beliefs about the relationship between an object and its surrounding actors is thus an attempt to predetermine the settings that users are asked to imagine' (Akrich, 1992: 208).

Not all programmes of action are equally strong. Some technologies inscribe weak/flexible programmes of action while others inscribe strong/inflexible programmes. The strength of inscriptions — whether they must be followed or can be avoided — depends on the *irreversibility* of the actor-network they are inscribed into (Callon, 1986: 211).

When studying the use of technical artifacts, one necessarily shifts back and forth 'between the designer's projected user and the real user' in order to describe this dynamically negotiated process of design (Akrich, 1992: 209). The inscribed patterns of use may not succeed because actual use deviates from the expected. Rather than following the assigned programme of action, a user may use the system in an unanticipated way: one may follow an anti-programme (Latour, 1991).

The strength of the inscription depends upon the functioning of the inscribed network. If the inscriptions are not similar to black boxes, and are less rigid and prone to manipulation, the network would not function as assumed. Inscriptions are used to turn artifacts into black boxes that enable the actors to achieve their goals more efficiently.

Black boxes are networks when 'many elements are made to act as one' or 'they are taken for granted'. They can be objects, people or networks. A stabilised network becomes a black box. As noted by Latour, when a machine runs efficiently, when a matter of fact is settled, one need focus only on its inputs and outputs and not on its internal complexity (Latour, 1987). Latour gives an example of a car as a black box: one need not look into its engine etc., as long as it functions well.

A stabilised network arises when translation is successful, where the alignment of interests of the actors in the network results from the enrolment of the actors. Each process of negotiation leads to displacement in the network that affects the actants as well as the actants of related networks. 'Destabilised networks' occur when networks are adapting to a consequent redistribution of power[1] by a change in the original goals of the network or as a result of other factors in which the alignment of the involved actors shifts, or when the actors are not authentically involved (derived by Rhodes, 2005, from Latour, 1987).

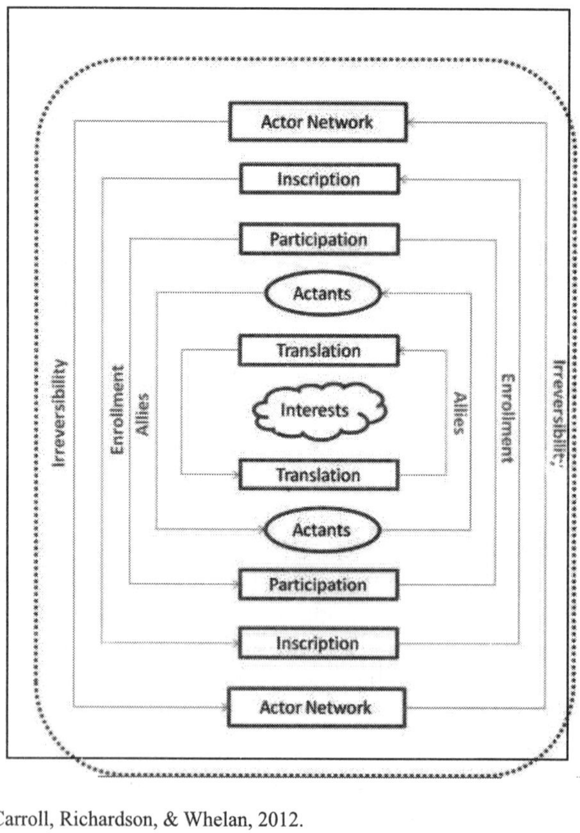

Source: Carroll, Richardson, & Whelan, 2012.

Fig. 2.1: Process of Irreversibility

As presented in Figure 2.1, Carroll, Richardson and Whelan (2012) explain that the creation and maintenance of actor-network centres on one single factor, namely 'interests:' of the primary actor and those of other actors. Motivated by their interests, the primary actor sets the action in motion. Through a series of translations, the actor-network is formed. Enrolment and inscription is used to stabilise the network. These processes form the network into what becomes known as the actor-network, which is irreversible and with which one cannot explore alternative opportunities at this point, i.e. the actor-network becomes a black box (Carroll, Richardson & Whelan, 2012).

The concept of irreversibility is described by Callon (1991) in 'Techno-Economic Networks and Irreversibility.' It is related to the degree to which a network can be said to have converged. Irreversibility refers to "the extent to which it is subsequently impossible to return to a point where that translation was only one amongst others; and the extent to which it shapes and determines subsequent translations" (Callon, 1991: 159).

2.3.2.3 *Delegation and Distribution of Agency*

Agency is defined as the capacity of an actor (agent) to 'modify a state of affairs by making a difference' (Latour, 2005: 71). In ANT, both humans and non-humans have agency, i.e. they are active, vibrant and exert power. According to the ANT perspective, agency 'is not an exclusive property of human beings, objects too have agency' (Latour, 2005: 63) cited in (Nimmo, 2011: 111). ANT thus extends agency beyond human intentionality. Such a claim asserts that what matters is not the intentionality itself, but how intentionality is shaped (allowed, encouraged, blocked, rendered possible) by an extension of causal relations between humans and non-humans (Dwiartama & Rosin, 2014: 3).

'Delegation' describes the interchangeability of the roles of a human and of the technical world in the network. An actor may achieve the intended goal in the network through either technical or social means. Latour and Johnson analysed various networks of door-closers using various combinations involving humans and non-humans (Latour & Johnson, 1988). The function or the role of both remains the same, although they are interchangeable. Although the primary set of actors had a defined role for the job, both had their own set of pros and cons in terms of functions. It is the prerogative of the primary actors to choose as to whom to delegate the work. Thus, in a complex network in the real world, the distinction between the social and the technical diminishes.

The mediating role technologies play illustrates how several day-to-day artifacts in life can be designed to shape human behaviour. Illustrating the delegation of agency through examples of door-closers and speed breakers, Latour and Johnson (1988) note that often non-humans are more predictable than humans in a network, and the processes which are governed by non-humans are more stable than the same processes which are governed by humans. They argue that 'artifacts can be deliberately designed to both replace human action and constrain and shape the actions of other humans,' and that 'understanding how technologies shape our everyday lives' is essential to understand the functioning of societies. Whether it is called translation, mediation or inscription, the process through which non-humans acquire tremendous importance in social life is the gradual shift in the type of links between entities from 'a provisionally less reliable one to a longer-lasting, more faithful one' (Latour & Johnson, 1988: 271).

The question that remains is whether or not artifacts delegate capacities or tasks back to humans. Referring to crashes of F-16 military aircraft, the search for human and technical causes, and the related distribution of accountability, Harbers (2005) dedicated his book *Inside the Politics of Technology: Agency and Normativity in the Co-production* to illustrate three central issues. The first relates to the proposition that in the co-production of science, technology and society, humanity and technology are mutually dependent. The second issue is the problem of agency, i.e. the role of human and non-human agents in the process of co-production. The major question revolves around agency, agents of co-production, liability, accountability, and the attribution and distribution of responsibilities. The third is the problem of normativity. While the heterogeneous nature of the network and the co-production theory are widely accepted, there is still contestation regarding the delegation of agency to non-humans and the distribution of agency between various actors. Harbers (2005) argues that the delegation of agency is a two-way process. In short, we move from a notion of non-human agency as an effect of human attributions of agency to artifacts, towards a notion of agency that is inseparable from the distribution of action across heterogeneous materials (Shiga, 2007: 46).

Actor-network theory asserts that agency is not an a priori given feature of an actor but is the outcome of interactions between the heterogeneous actors in the network. The notion of 'distributed agency' emphasises that agency is not located in an individual actor but is distributed among diverse (human and non-human) actors that jointly form a collective actor (Gomart & Hennion, 1999, as cited in Harbers, 2005: 86).

An actor, regardless of size, complexity or species, begins to acquire agency (capacities to perform a list of actions) through the primary translation mechanism in which a principal actor forms associations with other entities (Latour, 1987, as cited in Shiga, 2007: 44). The idea of a heterogeneous, or socio-technical network can subsequently be used to describe everything. This is another of the radical moves that ANT makes, arguing that everything — people, organisations, technologies, nature, politics, social orders — is the result, or effect, of heterogeneous networks.

Extending these arguments, Actor-Network theorists argue that the role of non-humans is not merely as instruments in the hands of humans. Neither human nor non-human actors can act independently of each other. Instead, they form heterogeneous networks. It is important that attempts to understand socio-technical dynamics examine how decisions emerge out of interactions amongst these collective actors.

2.4 Discussion

The section above presents an overview of ANT. The theory is about the formation of actor-networks, in which both human and non-human partake. It posits innovation "as a process of translation by which a vague initial idea is shaped, diverted and consolidated, to build up a network of allies who believe in test, and carry forward the development of the innovation" (Latour, 1987, as cited in Arnaboldi & Spiller, 2011: 641). The three critical concepts of ANT — translation, inscription, and delegation and distribution of agency — have been discussed. This research adopts these as analytical tools to understand the development of the BRTS project in Ahmedabad.

The translation process is all about an attempt by primary actors to translate the interests of others to match those of their own. This process of building actor-networks is multi-sided and contested. It involves displacing the existing, and attempting to prevent the other new. In this process, resistance to change is inevitable, as also is the competition from the other potential 'new,' which may not be under consideration. The resistances to change are "not accidental and unfortunate phenomena...but only regular manifestations of innovations interfering with stakeholders: interference occurs even in cases of seemingly 'incremental' innovation" (Pel, 2012: 1). Avoiding interference to overcome resistance is a preferred strategy of project proponents. Therefore, resistance management has been considered as key for successful translation. The effort in this research is to gain insights into the translation process and specifically the resistance management strategies adopted by the project planners in developing the BRTS in Ahmedabad.

From the discussion above, it is evident that instability is inherent in the innovation process. Focal actors attempt to make it stable through the delegation of agency to non-humans. In line with the programme of actions of BRTS-Ahmedabad, scripts are evolved and inscribed into these artifacts to modulate human behaviour and also make actor-networks durable.

Delegation of agency to non-humans makes the network stronger and more stable. Agency is delegated through inscriptions. A series of questions (Callon, 1986: 211) are raised to understand the role of non-humans in building actor-networks.

- Which programme of action is to be inscribed?
- Who inscribes it and how is it to be inscribed?
- Can the users alter it during use?
- What are the successive inscriptions?
- How strong is the inscription?

Actor-network theory asserts that agency is not an a priori given feature of an actor but is the outcome of interactions between the heterogeneous actors in the network. The notion of 'distributed agency' emphasises that agency is not located in an individual actor but is distributed among diverse (human and non-human) actors that jointly form a collective actor (Gomart & Hennion, 1999, as cited in Harbers, 2005: 86). Extending this further, it is argued that the decisions are not made based on a rational logical reasoning but emerge out of network interactions. This research focuses on delegation and distribution of agency to analyse how decisions evolved in deciding on various aspects of develpoing the BRTS.

2.4.1 Advantages and Limitations of the ANT Framework

There are several advantages as well as limitations of using ANT as an analytical framework for the study.

This study is inspired by the works of Scott-Smith (2013) and Valderrama and Jorgenson (2010). Scott-Smith (2013) based their research on a 1970s development project that involved the extraction of protein from plant leaves to provide nutritional supplement for diets in Nigeria. It identifies the main advantages and drawbacks of ANT as a way of examining development projects.

A major disadvantage is that ANT does not offer 'an all-encompassing theory, a grand narrative, or a set of revolutionary or replicable causes of success or failure' and, as noted by the authors, none exist. It is not that the ANT just offers 'a patient, painstakingly detailed description' which is, of course, a major advantage as it allows us to go beyond the state aims, objectives etc. It also looks at broader contexts and actors who contribute to the process of development. It thus provides us with a tool, 'black-box,' which enables us to dissect the complex world part by part.

ANT adopts a stance of amorality in its analysis of project success, which has been described as a major drawback. To quote an example, in the case of India's family planning practice in the 1970s, researchers suggest that the successful alliances which made the project need not have been morally correct. They also highlight that building alliances by 'not challenging the powerful structures and actors' is not the right approach. Instead, we need to bring them on board.

Valderrama and Jorgenson (2010) adopted the ANT approach for their research on 'The Design of Large Technological Systems — The Cases of Transmilenio in Bogotá and Metro in Copenhagen.' This researcher, while adopting the approach for his doctoral research, also notes certain limitations.

Although the proponents of ANT (Callon, 1986: 23, 25; Callon and Law, 1988: 292) claim that no hierarchy should be maintained between the actors beforehand, their analytical selection does privilege and construct a central actor, a choice that should be admitted upfront, just as Callon himself proposes in another study (Callon, 1986a).

Further, Valderrama and Jorgenson (2010) identify four other counts on which the ANT falls short: the roles of markets; actors' transformation and resistance; roles of users; and role of big politics. The argument is that big transport projects compete *for* the market and *in* the market and hence they are not judged in the marketplace; the assumption is that actors do not resist stubbornly, while users' role is not included and the role of big politics is completely missing.

2.4.2 Rationale for Adopting ANT Framework to Explain Large-Scale Project Development

In order to address complex socio-technical development processes, it is important to understand and appreciate that today, a hybrid of human and non-human elements proliferate. In fact, as Walsham (1997) has pointed out, the boundaries between the technical and the social on the one hand, and between human and machine capabilities on the other, are frequently contested and often negotiated. It is in this context that the actor-network theory has come to be a useful tool to illuminate the results of field research while providing a conceptual framework.

Actor-network theory is both theory and methodology combined, according to Walsham (1997). Therefore, it not only provides theoretical concepts, but also suggests, in an impartial manner, the elements that need to be traced.

The author is of the opinion that this aspect of ANT is unlike many social theories that allow the documentation of network elements even while facilitating analyses of various processes of implementation. Thus, in this thesis, ANT has been used as a theoretical framework. One advantage of using ANT as a framework is that it allows the addressing of local, yet broad social and economic structures that impact the processes chosen for the implementation of a project.

Heeks and Stanforth (2015) also offer a case study which leads them to conclude that ANT has been able to highlight the relationship between technology and development. They also argue that ANT has proved to be innovative in addressing some of the dichotomous situations stemming from non-linear processes, impacts and outcomes. This has been a subject of debate for a very long time, and one could argue that ANT-based accounts are neither unique, nor do they explain dualistic and asymmetrical issues and situations.

As Heeks and Stanforth (2015) point out, there are some challenges in applying ANT, and the present study attempts to address both the methodological limitations and analytical challenges. The major concern in the current research, however, is the explanation of the trajectory of technology and development.

Cresswell *et al.* (2010) also argue that an ANT-based approach can prove helpful in understanding how social effects are generated due to associations between different actors in a network. It is perhaps this aspect that prompted Walsham (1997) and Heeks and Stanforth (2015) to indicate that the utility of ANT is that it allows us to eventually understand the impact of complex actor-network interactions on social processes. ANT has also been found to be helpful in investigating technology implementations in sectors such as healthcare, and even in bringing about technical change. It is important to note that besides its applications, ANT has also stimulated an academic debate through its conceptualisation of the relationship between humans and technological objects. These aspects notwithstanding, the ANT approach is used in the present thesis for its ability to inform both processes and outcomes.

NOTE

1. Rather than power as possession, power is persuasion, 'measured' *via* the number of entities networked. Power is generated in a relational and distributed manner as a consequence of ordering struggles. Central to ordering struggles is the concept of displacement, inherent in the process of translation (Ritzer, 2005: 2).

3
Competitors as Collaborators
Mobilising Alliances Towards Successful Transit Development Projects

3.1 Introduction

The success or failure of development projects, in the eyes of the proponents of the *diffusion of innovation theory*, is assumed to be dependent on their inherent superior qualities (objectives) and planning and implementation practices. Negating this view, the actor-network theorists suggest an alternate view that projects succeed not because of their superior qualities but because of their ability to garner support from/mobilise alliance with relevant actors.

To put it in the words of Scott-Smith, the "development projects succeed or fail not on the basis of any inherent superiority or inferiority, but on the basis of the extent and durability of the alliances they create. This network of durable, extensive alliances explains the success of a project, and is not a mere product of the project's inherent value or validity. Furthermore, this network of alliances is created not because a project is 'right' or 'wrong,' but because people and things are convinced that the project can advance their own interests, according to the role in the project they have been assigned" (Scott-Smith, 2013: 3).

Successful innovation means formation of strong and durable actor-networks. Actor-networks are formed through the process of *translation*; translation of an actor's interests to match the interests of that of the focal actors/project designers. These translations are made durable through the involvement of non-human actors. The innovation process, however, is a multi-sided and contested process. As it involves displacing the existing order, resistance to change is inevitable. Also adding to the resistance is the competition from the other potential 'new,' which is not under consideration.

As presented in Chapter 2, the translation process involves four moments: Problematisation, Interessement, Enrolment and Mobilisation.

- At the *problematisation* stage, the prime actor attempts to define the problem such that other actors perceive it as their problem and thereby the prime actor becomes indispensable and assumes the role of the Obligatory Passage Point.
- At the *interessement* stage, the primary actors seek to convince other actors to agree on and accept the definition of the primary actor.
- *Enrolment* is the negotiation phase wherein the roles of actors are defined and enacted.
- *Mobilisation* means that negotiations in the network have been successful and the network has stabilised. Failing to mobilise means actors have betrayed and failed to act out the agreed role.

Through application of the ANT concept of 'translation,' this chapter presents Ahmedabad's BRT project development process. Specifically, it seeks to gain an insight into the following:

(i) How did the idea of BRTS gain acceptance in Ahmedabad? Did the existing and the potential competitors resist the idea? How was the resistance overcome?

(ii) The actors who come into play during implementation are a different set who will resist the 'new,' as change from the existing is perceived to cause displacement and thus leads to resistance. How was such resistance overcome ?

(iii) With the passage of time, in a dynamic environment, the new actor has matured and so also the old has transformed, and some may have vanished. New actors may have emerged. The power equations would have changed, calling for (re)translation for the 'new' to exist and grow. The third part of the narrative is 'how did this happen?'

The narrative in this chapter is based on the researcher's first-hand experience, interviews with stakeholders and select archival sources. This chapter has been divided into four parts. The section above restated the theoretical context and specific questions attempted to be answered in this chapter. In Section 2, Ahmedabad's explorations to search for a superior (rapid) transit alternative have been presented. Section 3 presents a chain of translations and retranslation processes which have taken place in Ahmedabad towards implementing the BRTS specifically addressing the three questions above. Section 4 summarises the discussion.

3.2 Evolution of Ahmedabad's Transit System — Ahmedabad Municipal Transport Services

This section briefly dwells on the efforts made in the city of Ahmedabad to develop transit systems and summarises the status of transit in Ahmedabad around the time the BRTS project was being conceived.

City bus services were operational in Ahmedabad during the pre-independence period. These were operated by three private companies: Morris Transport Company, Ahmedabad Bus Corporation and Munishi Bus Services. In 1946, however, the bus services were discontinued due to communal riots in the city. This led the Ahmedabad Municipality to take up the responsibility of operating transit services.

In 1947, with a fleet of 60 buses, Ahmedabad Municipality established Ahmedabad Municipal Transport Services (AMTS) to operate a city bus service. The status of Ahmedabad Municipality was elevated to that of a Municipal Corporation in 1950. As per the provisions of the Bombay Provincial Municipal Corporation Act (1949), providing transport services was a discretionary service of the municipal corporation. AMTS was established as a new body under the Act.

AMTS is under the administrative control of a statutory body, namely the Transport Committee, formed by the General Board of the Ahmedabad Municipal Corporation (AMC). Its financial control lies with the General Board of the AMC. The Transport Committee comprises nine members, including the Chairman. They are drawn from various fields, one of them being AMC's Standing Committee Chairman. These members need not necessarily be elected Municipal Councillors.

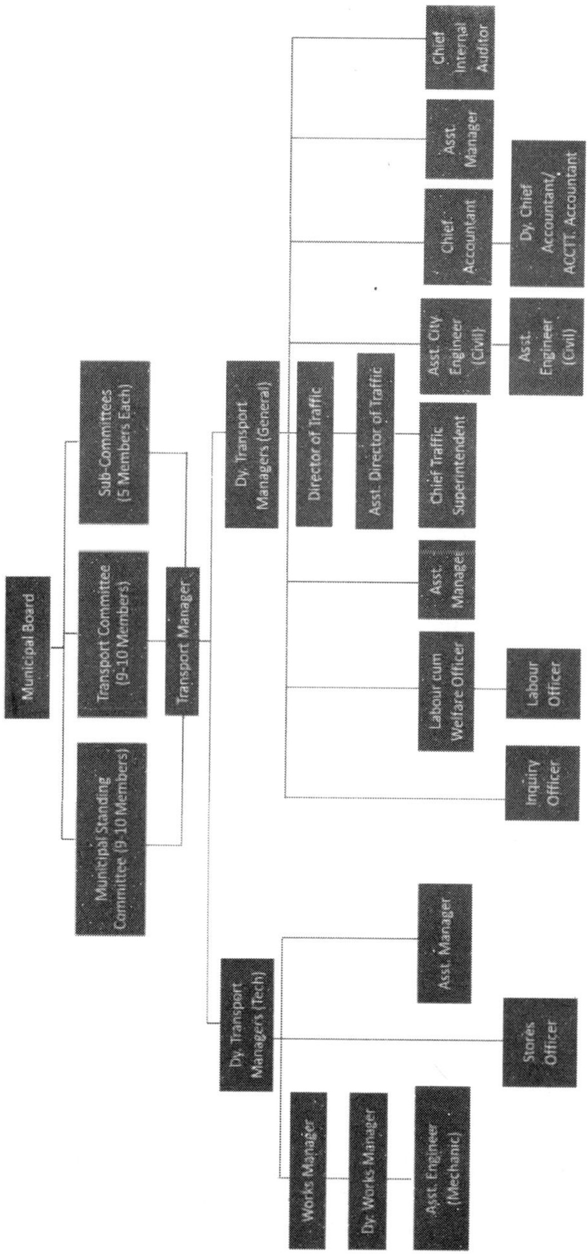

Fig. 3.1: AMTS Organisation Structure

A 'Transport Manager' — generally, one of the Deputy Municipal Commissioners — is given the charge of exercising all administrative and operational powers under the control and supervision of Transport Committee, and heads the administration of AMTS. The Transport Manager, however, is not a member of the Transport Committee.

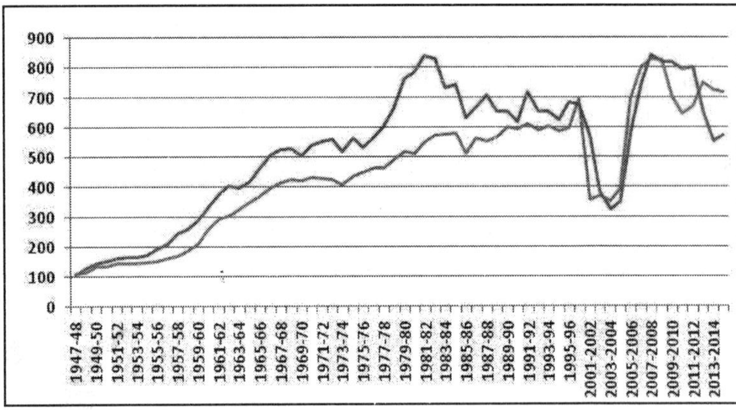

Source: AMTS (2015).

Fig. 3.2: AMTS Fleet and Ridership Growth

As Figure 3.2 shows, until the 1980s, AMTS experienced consistent growth, both in fleet size and in ridership. During 1981-82, AMTS, with about 550 buses, carried 0.84 million passengers everyday. Since then, the ridership has declined steadily. In 2004-05, the ridership was down to only 350 thousand passengers a day. The fleet, too, had come down to about 450 buses. With consistent efforts, mainly as a part of the BRTS development initiative, there has been an increase in the fleet size. But the ridership, though having marginally recovered, continues to be low.

A rapid rise in personalised vehicles during the 1980s is one of the main causes for the decline in public transport in the city. As noted in the DPR (AMC, 2006: 3-1), at the time of formation of the state of Gujarat in 1961, there were only 43,000 private vehicles registered in Ahmedabad. This figure rose to over 70 lakh by 2004, recording a 160-fold rise in four decades. In Ahmedabad district, a total of 14.9 lakh motor vehicles were registered in 2004, as against a mere 63,000 in 1971. Of the total vehicles in 2004, 73 per cent were two wheelers. The district, which accommodates 11 per cent of the state population, accounts for about 21 per cent of the vehicles registered in the state[1].

This rapid growth of vehicles has led to the worsening of the situation for public transport to a significant extent (AMC, 2006: 1).

On the other hand, AMTS as an organisation was going through difficulties due to financial constraints and frequent demands from the labour unions for increased wages etc. AMTS has no capital base and AMC provides financial assistance to it, as and when required, in the form of interest-bearing loans (AMC, 2006). The losses of AMTS have been increasing year after year (see Figure 3.3). A case was registered in 2000 by the labour unions for their pending demand to regularise *ad hoc* employees. AMTS found it difficult to abosrb more people as the wage and retirement benefits were already very high (Vora, 2014).

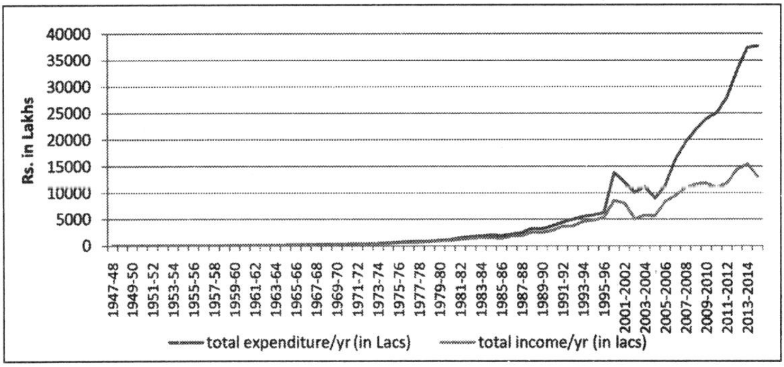

Source: AMTS (2015).

Fig. 3.3: AMTS Revenue and Expenditure (in lakhs)

To sum up, around the time when the BRTS project was conceived, the public transport services in the city of Ahmedabad were inadequate and poor.

Past Efforts to Introduce Metro and BRTS

As per old records available with the Ahmedabad Urban Development Authority, an attempt was made in 1984 and a feasibility study was initiated by RITES, but no further decision was taken at that particular time. By the 1990s, Curitiba's bus system innovations had become a success story and several international agencies including the World Bank were promoting the priority bus idea. The idea was then known as Bus Ways and not BRTS. During the same time, a master's thesis was undertaken at CEPT University on introducing bus lanes in Ahmedabad. With the initiative of AMC, AMTS assigned a study to Pallavan Transport Corporation to look into the feasibility of developing bus lanes on Ashram Road. The findings of the study, however, were not in favour doing so (AMTS, 1996). The potential traffic conflicts which looked to be unresolvable were identified as the major difficulty in implementing the bus lanes (Patel V. L., 2015).

A more systematic effort was initiated by the Government of Gujarat (GoG) through the Gujarat Infrastructure Development Board (GIDB) in 1997. A large consultancy assignment valued at INR 7 crore was commissioned to study and develop a strategy to resolve the emerging transport problems of Ahmedabad. The study titled 'Integrated Public Transportation System Plan' was assigned to Louis Berger Associates based on a global competitive selection process. The study, on behalf of the Government of Gujarat, was monitored by a team of experts from CEPT. A Steering Committee was formed to oversee the project development under the chairmanship of Principal Secretary, Urban Development, GoG. The terms of reference of the study required an integrated approach to transit development. Land use and transport and modal integration were both part of the scope. Further, the study was mode neutral, and was divided into two phases. The first phase consisted of preparation of a Strategic Plan. In the second stage, a Detailed Project Report was to be prepared for developing rapid transit system on a pilot corridor.

The study took longer than expected, and the first phase report was submitted in 2002. Based on the discussions with GIDB, while the strategies suggested were, on the whole, in the right direction, the consultant's recommendation to develop metro rail on a 10 km network as pilot, was not found to be acceptable by the Government of Gujarat.

Summing up

A series of efforts to develop quality transit were initiated by the state and local government from time to time, and some of the major ones have been narrated above. But none of these could fructify, or to put it in ANT parlance, these were failed problematisations. The studies were initiated, detailed assessments were undertaken and proposals were worked out, but in the end, the focal actor(s) failed to define the problem such that others could relate to it and join the network. It is against this background that the new initiative began in 2005.

3.3 Current Effort to Develop Rapid Transit Systems: Translation Process

The search for transit solutions continued through the years. The Government of Gujarat observed 2005 as the 'Urban Development Year,' and it undertook several focused initiatives to resolve infrastructural issues of Ahmedabad and other cities of Gujarat. Urban transport received high priority among these initiatives. The decision to build metro rail and BRTS in Ahmedabad was taken by the Hon. Chief Minister as part of the Urban Development Year-2005 initiatives.

Project development was not a linear process moving from one stage to another. It experienced several challenges which are narrated below in three parts. The account presented here, however, does not include every single move by every actor. The narration is limited to three major aspects of the project, which adequately explain the development process.

3.3.1 *Converting Competitors into Collaborators: Making BRTS an Acceptable Idea*

At the stage when the idea of BRTS was being considered, a series of actors were identified as potential competitors. Some of them already existed, while others were likely to emerge. This section deals with the actors and their role in making the BRT idea acceptable (or otherwise).

The Government of Gujarat initiated the project. Two agencies — Urban Development Department (UDD) and the Gujarat Infrastructure Development Board (GIDB) — were active participants in initiating the idea.

GIDB is a special purpose vehicle chaired by the Chief Minister. It has a specific mandate to promote private participation in infrastructure development in the state. In 2004, GIDB had invited the then Managing Director of Delhi Metro Rail Corporation (DMRC) for a presentation on the Ahmedabad-Gandhinagar Metro proposal. The presentation was made to the Hon. Chief Minister of Gujarat. In addition to senior officers of the Government of Gujarat, a few academicians and professionals were also invited. During the discussion, the issue of financial sustainability of the metro rail system came up. After the meeting, the need for sustainable alternatives was also discussed.

As a follow-up to this meeting, in early 2005, the GIDB issued two work orders: one to DMRC for preparing a 'Detailed Project Report for Ahmedabad-Gandhinagar Metro Rail Project' and the second to the CEPT University for undertaking a feasibility study of Ahmedabad BRTS. With this as the beginning, the idea of BRTS for Ahmedabad took shape, and gradually developed physically into a reality.

Ahmedabad Municipal Corporation (AMC) is the prime mover of the project, and has a mandate to provide public transport as a discretionary service. The project is housed in its jurisdiction, and has been and will be further implemented on AMC roads.

CEPT University, Ahmedabad has been extending its technical support to national, state and local governments mainly in the areas related to habitat. CEPT's interest was to work with cities and states to turn theories into facts and vice versa. While the CEPT was officially assigned with the role of a design consultant, the AMC and other authorities considered CEPT as their technical partner.

As presented above, initially, the GIDB was entrusted with the project planning, design and development decisions. As mentioned by Mukim (2015), once the JnNURM was announced, the GoG decided to submit the project for funding under the JnNURM. With the changed funding strategy, AMC took on the role of a principal decision maker. The technical support from CEPT continued. The GIDB contract with CEPT ended and the AMC signed a new agreement with an expanded scope. Given the newness of the concept, the AMC expected CEPT to play a more active and involved role as a technical partner.

3.3.1.1 *Translation—Competing Actors and their Interests*

The Ahmedabad Municipal Transport Service, the proposed metro rail system and the shared auto-rickshaw were the modes in direct competition with the proposed BRTS for providing transit services in the city.

Ahmedabad Municipal Transport Service (AMTS) is a body of the AMC, established to provide transit services in the city. At the time when BRTS was being conceived, AMTS was under threat of closure due to poor service, labour unrest and poor financial condition. It did see BRTS as a competitor but was weak as an opponent as it depended on the AMC for financial support. Survival and staying relevant were the primary concerns of AMTS.

Shared Auto-Rickshaws: The trend to provide transit services provided through three wheeled auto-rickshaws as an informal public transit system in the city started during the early part of the 1980s. After the closure of textile mills in Ahmedabad, many workers found it fascile to enter the labour market by becoming auto-rickshaw drivers. This form of transit supply is illegal as it often carries more people than the designed capacity of the vehicle, apart from being unsafe and polluting. It also poses a threat to the long-term development of a formal transit system. With the decline of AMTS, the role of shared auto-rickshaws rose and had become a major provider of transit by 2004-05. It was expected that these operators would prevent any effort that might take away their share of the market. As they were illegal, they focused on whatever best they could do to maximise their revenue when things stood in their favour.

Metro Rail System: The discussion on metro rail has been going on for long (Global Mass Transit, 2010). The Delhi Metro opened in 2002. The project was completed within budget and three years ahead of schedule. It is also one of the fastest metro constructions achieved in the world. Given this background, a metro rail system has become an aspiration of the people. Hence, metro rail was a mode which found itself in competition with BRTS for the space in the rapid transit market.

Developing a **Suburban Rail Transit System** along existing rail lines to connect the city with its industrial suburbs such as Kalol, Naroda, Mehmedabad had also been under discussion.

People and their Representatives (Politicians) are important stakeholders. People would be interested in benefiting from the investments being made part of project development. The people's representatives (councillors) are interested in taking credit for bringing projects (investments) to the area which they represent.

Figure 3.4 presents the key actors, their goals/interests and the issues they are concerned with which are likely to influence their decision in participation in the network.

3.3.1.2 *The Process of Translation: Converting Competition to Collaboration*

The translation of the competing interests to align with the designer's interest has been a multi-strategy dynamic process.

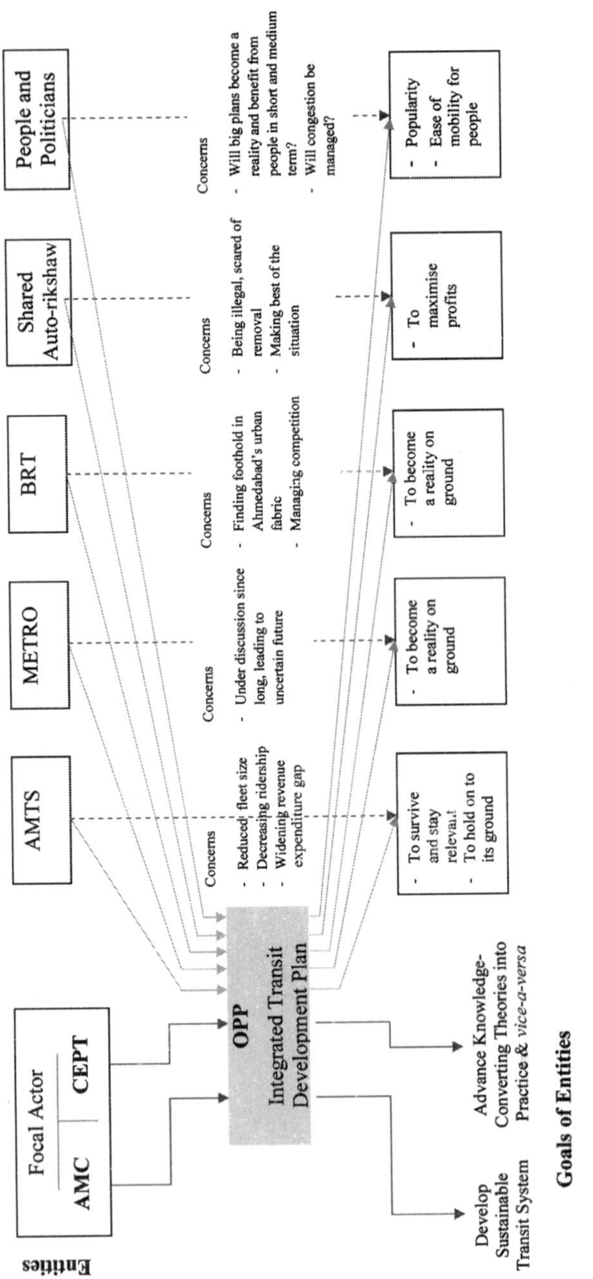

Fig. 3.4: Elements of Translation — Converting Competitors into Collaborators, 2005

Problematisation

While *problematising,* the focal actors attempt to define the problem such that other actors perceive it as their problem and thereby the prime actor becomes indispensable and assumes the role of the Obligatory Passage Point. In many ways, problematisation was already in place, with the state (GIDB[2] and the Chief Minister) deciding to adopt a multi-modal transit system. As noted in the DPR (AMC, 2006), the plan was titled Integrated Public Transport System Plan, and the BRTS development was thus part of a larger plan. The DPR clearly states "that no single mode would cater to the mobility needs of the city and that the 'bus' forms the most critical segment of the public transport system in the city" (AMC, 2006: 2). To quote the then Chief Minister, "To translate our big dreams into reality and put Gujarat's developmental process on a higher trajectory, we need to build on our existing strengths; we need to adopt multiple solutions to meet the needs of multi-cultural and diverse socio-economic context, and we also need to look at options as an integrated whole" (AMC, 2006).

Thus, the focal actors decided the problem: If the problems of transport had to be resolved, the city needed to develop an integrated transport system in which a bus system, in general, and BRT, in particular, would have a central role.

As highlighted in the first newsletter of Ahmedabad BRT (February 2006), "the recent initiative ... to develop BRTS is in recognition of the fact that no single mode will completely serve the accessibility and mobility needs of the city, and the bus system, both in its basic form (regular bus) and rapid form (BRTS), makes it a critical and major component in an integrated transit system of any mega city" (CEPT, AMC, AUDA, GIDB, 2005).

With this as the basis, the focal actors elaborated on the components required to develop and implement an integrated public transit system plan, which included (AMC, 2006):

- A suburban rail transit system to connect the city with its industrial suburbs such as Kalol, Naroda, Mehmedabad etc.
- A metro rail system to cater to major high-intensity movement within and between the city and Gandhinagar.
- A Bus Rapid Transit System to cater to high density mobility needs of the city.

- A regular bus system to support the BRTS.
- Decentralised regional bus and rail terminals.
- Auto-rickshaws as last-mile connectors.
- Integration of different forms of systems, i.e. BRT and other urban transport systems, with bicycles and pedestrian facilities.
- Integration of Land Use and Transport Elements (with increased FSI along the BRTS corridor).

By adopting a broad-based definition of the problem, the focal actors were able to capture the attention and interest of the competitors. In this way, the focal actors and their definition of an integrated transit system became the obligatory passage point.

Interessement Leading to Enrolment

While the broad definition of the problem (in this case, the integrated transit plan) outlined was adequate to evince the interest of competitors, it was not adequate enough to persuade them to accept it. This involved a series of interessement mechanisms to coax them into the project, i.e. to make them agree to the roles defined by the focal actor. At the *interessement* stage, the focal actors exert influence over other actors to agree to and accept the definition of the problem. Persuasion uses various devices/mechanisms. Project planners used both broad-based mechanisms to mobilise general public opinion and political commitment. Some mechanisms were focused specifically on the competitors. Once successful, the ones who are persuaded are locked into the project, which means they are enrolled.

Steering Committee: A formal approval for the project was necessary. A Steering Committee under the chairmanship of Secretary, Urban Development was set up with the Ahmedabad Municipal Commissioner, Chief Executive Officers of AUDA and GIDB, and Secretary Expenditure as members to monitor the progress of the project.

Public Consultations: A series of public consultations were held through workshops, lectures, road shows etc. The first major workshop with about 165 participants from different walks of life was held on August 25, 2005, and it gave the city an overview of the BRTS. The workshop participants included all the stakeholders including the AMTS, the auto-rickshaw association, the city traffic police etc. The newsletter, which was brought out after the workshop, carried a message from the Hon. Chief Minister, and was an assurance of the political sanction and commitment to the project. This workshop was followed by meetings of the Directors of premier institutions located in Ahmedabad, which brought in the approval of the intellectual capital of the city. Various road shows as part of a bi-annual vibrant summit and lectures at various colleges were also effective communication mechanisms (Swamy, 2010).

Formal Approvals to the Plan: With the announcement of the JnNURM, the AMC decided to take the project to the Ministry of Urban Development (MoUD), Government of India, for funding support. Approvals from the local body and the state government were taken before forwarding it to the MoUD. Being the first of its kind, the proposal went through several iterations before it was approved. With funding support assured, the acceptability of the plan got further enhanced.

Formation of AJL: Ahmedabad Janmarg Limited (AJL), a fully-owned company of the AMC, was set up to manage BRTS operations in the city. So as to get support from various stakeholders, the company board was broad-based. It was headed by the Municipal Commissioner and included the mayor, the standing committee chairman, the transport committee chairman, the opposition leader, the AJL CEO as well as the traffic police. This body took all decisions regarding AJL's operations and brought about coordination with the AMTS.

The following were the persuasive mechanisms specially directed towards competitors.

Para-transit Initiatives: Placing regulatory restrictions on auto-rickshaws, though feasible, was difficult to implement as it was not always acceptable to political entities and communities. To overcome the obstacles, a two-pronged strategy was adopted.

Developmental Mechanisms: In 2005, based on the annual air quality monitoring exercise undertaken by the Central Pollution Control Board, Ahmedabad was rated as the fourth most polluted city in the country. As a response, the first step the city took was to convert the auto-rickshaws, a prevalent para-transit mode, from petrol to CNG, and to deregister vehicles that had been registered before 1991. By the end of 2006, more than 44,000 auto-rickshaws and buses were converted to CNG. The success of this effort was mainly due to the fact that the relevant stakeholders were taken on board in the decision-making process, and the para-transit operators were given support to access bank loans for procuring new vehicles or for converting them from petrol to CNG. The pricing of CNG *vis-à-vis* petrol was also such that it was beneficial to convert to CNG. The plan also included providing parking facilities near bus stations as a step towards integration of para-transit as a feeder system (Gautam, 2010).

Additionally, auto-rickshaws were provided with designated parking places as part of BRT street design. This was done for the first time in Ahmedabad.

Market Mechanisms: Given the widespread use of auto-rickshaws, market mechanism was used to alter their operational strategy. As part of BRTS trial runs (Swamy, 2010), BRT buses were plying on the first 12.5 km route and offered free service to the public for three months (Desh Gujarat, 2009). Though, initially the service was limited in terms of schedules and duration, with growing popularity, fullscale service was soon started. These trials had multiple objectives:

(a) to test the infrastructure,
(b) to familiarise people with the use of BRTS,
(c) to attract passengers on board with a view to develop habit formation, and last, but not the least,
(d) to stop the viability of shared auto-rickshaws.

As auto-rickshaws were not in a position to compete with the BRTS, which began offering service free of charge, they were forced to become a feeder service. This was how the para-transit, which had been serving as an 'informal transit' system, was *enrolled* to be BRTS's feeder.

AMTS City Bus System

As stated before, in the early part of the decade beginning 2001, public transport services in the city of Ahmedabad were inadequate and poor. The supply was characterised by inadequate and aged fleet, large number of routes and destination-oriented route structure focused on the central part of the city. The aged fleet not only made the services unreliable due to frequent breakdowns, but also added to deteriorating air quality. The decision making within the organisation was driven by AMC councillors, for whom adding a bus route was an easy way to increase patronage within their wards, thus contributing to the proliferation of routes. Too many routes and fewer buses meant very low frequency.

Developmental Actions: Three major areas of action were identified by the focal actors:

(i) To augment the fleet size through private participation.
(ii) To complement these, placing 530 buses (procured under the JnNURM by AJL) for operation with the AMTS.
(iii) To convert diesel-powered buses to CNG buses.

While augmenting the fleet, it was also decided that instead of AMTS directly procuring and operating the buses, a private operator would be involved. This was expected to bring efficiency in operations and not burden the city public transit authority with manpower-related and other associated long-term liabilities. The operator was to be paid on a per kilometre basis.[7] These initiatives have had a positive impact on air quality (reduced SPM levels) as well as improved transit ridership. Thirdly, AJL, the company running the BRT, procured 530 buses under the JnNURM and handed them over to AMTS for operations.

Operational Conditions: A set of operating conditions were put in place to enable the integrated transit system to function efficiently. The BRT in Ahmedabad was designed to operate as a 'closed system,' meaning that only BRT buses would ply in BRT corridors and would not move out. This meant that while AMTS services would be withdrawn from the corridor, it was also assured that the BRTS would not go beyond the corridor limits. AMTS would thus have about 500 km of the network for operating its services, while the BRTS would have 89 km. To make this work, several other mechanisms were also put in place as presented in Table 3.1.

Table 3.1: BRTS *vs.* AMTS Aspects

Sl. No.	Aspect	BRTS	AMTS
1	Service type	Closed	Open
2	Fare collection	Off-board automatic	On-board manual
3	Fare levels	1.5 times of AMTS	1
4	Bus door	On right hand side	On left hand side
5	Passenger Information System	On buses and stations	On buses only

The aspects mentioned in the table make each service operating outside their respective corridors a difficult proposition. Given the small fleet with the AMTS, they did not find it hard to accept these conditions. As discussed, steps such as supporting fleet augmentation, making AMTS part of the BRTS governing body and providing BRTS buses with right side doors were the key strategies adopted by the project proponents to enrol AMTS.

Metro System

In June 2005, DMRC submitted a detailed project report for a Metro Rail System between Ahmedabad and Gandhinagar. The report recommended a total of 43.5 km of network (north-south corridor of 32.66 km and east-west corridor over a length of 10.90 kms). As per the report, the system costs were estimated to be INR 5012 crore (i.e. INR 92 crore/km)(GIDB, 2005). The BRT DPR was finalised in September 2005. The metro alignment was kept intact as proposed in the metro DPR. As BRTS and metro were to be designed as complementary systems and not competitors, there was no reason for resistance from metro rail towards the proposal to build the BRTS.

Regional/Suburban Rail System

A proposal for a regional rail on the existing railway network cutting across the city was initiated in 2006 by AUDA. The project is still under discussion. As the alignment or funds of the Regional Rail were not in competition with the proposal of BRTS (one of the actors), the Regional Rail and the BRTS were not seen as being in competition with each other.

Summing up

From the narration above, it is clear that the focal actors were successful in converting competitors into its collaborators by adopting an accommodative approach. It redefined the roles of existing and potential competitors to match with its own project's interest. The redefined roles were made acceptable through various strategies that included accommodation, enticement, force etc.

3.3.1.3 *The Process of Translation: Widening the Base to Minimise the Resistance to Change*

In addition to the competing actors who were directly in competition with BRTS to provide transit service, there were others whose interests were being affected by the project directly or indirectly, significantly or marginally, and who were likely to interfere with the project development. The project planners needed to anticipate and be ready with strategies to minimise risk. These were mainly encountered during the project implementation stage. This section narrates the translation process.

Broad Basing the Project Scope

In 2005, the final decision of selecting a bus-based rapid transit as one of the primary public transit systems was taken by GIDB, chaired by the then Chief Minister of Gujarat. The Chief Minister's interest in the project was instrumental in the project promotion all through its development and even after operations began. The GIDB assigned the project to CEPT University in 2005.[3] A draft report was prepared in August, which was extensively discussed in a major consultative workshop held in the city later in the same month.

From the review of the DPR, it may be deciphered that Ahmedabad BRT planning has at least five distinguishable features that turned competitors into collaborators (AMC, 2006). These are:

(i) The plan was conceived of as an *integrated multi-modal transit system plan* rather than just a BRT development plan.
(ii) The plan proposed a *wider coverage of network* to distribute investment benefits and thereby mobilise larger sections of the society (including the political leadership).
(iii) The plan adopted a *complete network and complete street approach* with an effort to achieve system-wide optimisation rather than benefit maximisation.
(iv) The plan evolved through *participatory processes.*
(v) While the plan was inclusive, it also envisaged the development of infrastructure to provide exclusivity to the BRTS (*protective envelop*).

Each of these is presented below.

Integrated multi-modal transit system: The plan envisages the inclusion of proposals for integrating the metro rail system, proposed suburban rail system, BRTS, AMTS and para transit. Integration in terms of physical, institutional and fare systems was proposed.

Source: AMC, 2006.

Fig. 3.5: Integrated Multi-modal System

Wider Network Coverage: The BRT proposal included 155[4] km of BRTS network, of which 58 km was to be developed in the first phase, another 30 km in the second phase and the balance in third phase. The BRT system plan, as envisaged by the focal actors (AMC, 2006) was developed keeping the following as guiding principles:

- Given the low-levels of public transit patronage, the prime task of the initiative at the early stages was to develop a market for public transport.
- To keep a medium and long-term perspective.
- To choose options that were technically feasible to implement

(road width, corridor length, fewer bottlenecks—e.g. junctions and level crossings etc.).
- To minimise adverse environmental and social issues.
- To ensure system-wide impacts.

System-wide impacts included relief from congestion, improved safety, maximisation of ridership, serving the needs of the poor, providing opportunities for transit-oriented development, promoting the Compact City concept, and enabling integration with other modes. The expected (positive) impacts had to be city-wide and not just limited to specific areas. The selected plan covered about one-third of the population (including the student population) of Ahmedabad residing within walking distance of the Phase-1 corridor of 58 km. The corridor covered about 38 per cent of the total jobs located within walking distance of the Phase-1 corridor.

As outlined here, wider network coverage was meant to mobilise larger sections of the society as well as the political leadership. Innovation process is a 'multisided and contested' process. Thus, resistance to change is inevitable. It is believed that project planners, while designing/implementing the system, adopt strategies to minimise resistance and avoid interference. In contrast to this apparently logical approach, the project planners in Ahmedabad adopted strategies that instead invited interferences by adopting wide network coverage as an interference management strategy in the making of Janmarg.

According to the traditional approach, initiators of the innovation would adopt a 'pilot' approach wherein a corridor of manageable length, which is wider than 30/35 metres[5] is selected, designed, built and showcased so as to prove its usefulness. This 'success' is then attempted for replication in other parts of the city. However, the initiators of Janmarg discarded the 'pilot' approach as it was felt that in publicly funded projects, more resistance gets developed when it is piloted. Instead, it was decided to go with full-scale planning and implementation. Further, instead of selecting a corridor of manageable size, the initiators of Janmarg selected a large network of 155 km, of which the first phase was 58 km. In selecting the network, road width was taken into consideration but was not followed rigidly. Neither was traffic density taken into consideration. By widening the scope in terms of coverage, the focal actors invited interferences not just from stakeholders with direct interest but also from others.

Complete Network and Complete Streets Approach

By adopting a complete network and streets approach, the intention was to achieve system-wide optimisation rather than user benefit maximisation. The city has a well-structured ring-radial network. There were missing links (incomplete network because of missing links, i.e. bridges or railway line) that constrained the flow of traffic. As part of the 'complete network strategy' in the BRTS plan, the city built two river bridges, 10 rail-over bridges and 20 flyovers. These were strategically located, keeping in mind system optimisation and not just from a BRT perspective.

'The major conflicts at the city level are the conflicts related to road space use between different users. Except in Ahmedabad, all other BRT systems have been criticised in the local popular media for "taking away the road space from regular traffic." This clearly shows that urban opinion-making is hijacked by the vocal middle classes who are also the owners of PMT vehicles and who resist more equitable distribution of road space' (Mahadevia, Joshi, & Datey, 2013: 121).

Taking this into consideration, the city undertook measures to minimise the conflict by adding capacities to mixed carriageways. Of the total BRTS network, about 75 per cent of the BRT network was widened in terms of right of way or carriageway or both (Swamy, H. M., 2011). As a result, new capacities were created in the network. A part of the added capacity was drawn for BRT building. In essence, the mixed traffic lane users got back whatever road space they were using without the BRT buses coming in their way. As a result, in the short run, both the BRT and the mixed traffic benefited in terms of travel speed (Swamy, H.M., 2011). To enhance this further, the designers selected corridors such that they were 'connecting busy places while avoiding busy streets.' Connecting the areas of the urban poor was a key strategy of the complete network approach.

Ahmedabad city has potential land for development in prime locations within the inner CBD areas in the form of vacant mill land, open grounds etc. The routes were so chosen that the mass transit would act as a catalyst for area development along the corridors. The city is already witnessing mixed land use development along the corridors. This, in turn, is expected to keep the city compact and retain the short trip lengths of Ahmedabad.

To communicate the message of inclusiveness and people-centredness to the public, the system was named 'Janmarg,' meaning 'People's Way.' Figure 3.7 shows the design of the corridor that has central bus stations, exclusive BRT lanes, mixed traffic, bicycle lanes, footpaths, pedestrian crossings etc.

While the plan was accommodative of different interests, it also envisaged development of a *protective envelope for BRTS* through involvement of non-human actors.

Source: CoE-UT, CEPT.

Fig. 3.6: Corridor Design

Plan Evolution through Participatory Processes

The need for consultation was recognised, as the BRT system was new for citizens as well as other stakeholders. Starting from the initial planning to the implementation and operations of the project, consultations in the form of workshops, publications, media propagation and branding were explored. Workshops were conducted during the initial planning stages, which helped propagate BRT as a sustainable solution and brought about more clarity about the division of road space, exclusive bus lanes, median bus stations etc. To understand and explain how all this was supposed to work, delegates from the AMC visited other BRT cities such as London, Beijing, Bogota, Guangzhou, Singapore, Jakarta and Seoul.

The consultation aspect of the project took a serious step in August 2005, when an exclusive workshop was organised by the technical consultants with AMC, GIDB and AUDA. The workshop was centred on features of the project such as corridors and their selection, design of the system and its components, and implementation strategies. Feedback from the community and decision makers was the main outcome of the process. A decision on identifying private bus operators for the project was also on the agenda. This workshop was succeeded by another one in October of the same year, focusing on bus technology. Another aspect of the consultations was to engage with national and international transport experts. This was attempted through organising meetings and seminars on various aspects of BRTS planning and design.

In the case of Janmarg, the role played by the media in propagating the idea of BRTS among the public was vital in enhancing public outreach of the project. The media practised constructive criticism which not only influenced public opinion, but also helped the system to improvise and improve at each stage. The system design was also showcased widely through exhibitions such as the Real Estate Mega Show and other property expos within the state and at national and international conventions during 2007-09.

The consultations and public outreach during the implementation of the pilot corridor were crucial for the success of the BRTS project in Ahmedabad. The turning point of the project was the operation of the system free of charge for a period of three months. This gave the users the opportunity to understand the system through first-hand experience and to provide feedback. People from various social, economic, cultural and religious backgrounds were personally invited by the Municipal Commissioner and provided guided tours. School children, the visually impaired and the differently-abled citizens were also taken aboard the BRTS during this time. This offered the planners, operators and administrators the feedback and opportunity to rectify issues pertaining to scheduling, bus operations, and bus station and junction management prior to the system launch.

BRT was a system new to its commuters and other stakeholders. The feedback from various consultation processes facilitated knowledge exchange, clarification of BRT concepts, rectification of design and a rethink on strategies. This continues even till date through monthly surveys which take user feedback and suggestions and keep a check on system performance and maintenance. This was a key strategy that enabled the successful evolution of the system in Ahmedabad. The system was also given a brand value. It had a specially designed logo and a name, both of which were widely advertised. The elements of the system such as bus stations, buses, corridor, etc. had a unique aesthetic appeal and design. The logo for the system was designed by the prestigious National Institute of Design, which further contributed to broad-basing the stakes and mobilising credibility.

Protective Envelope Through Involvement of Non-human Actors

While the competition with the existing was to be avoided by including its interests as part of the plan, strategies to protect the new through a protective envelope developed around the system were critical for the innovation to succeed. Towards this end, the designers of Janmarg designed various non-human artifacts such that it got its exclusivity.

Physical Artifacts: Janmarg is a full BRT system, which has components that define its efficiency as a public transit mode. The various components of BRT include corridors, bus stations, vehicles, a fare collection system, an intelligent transport system, and a services and operations plan (refer Appendix 1). An exclusive corridor, high-platform buses, right-side door, external ticketing etc. are some of the strategies designed for Janmarg. These are discussed in greater detail in the next chapter.

Institutional Arrangements: Additionally, a new entity, Ahmedabad Janmarg Limited (AJL), was created as a special purpose vehicle under the Companies Act. It is fully owned by the local government, AMC, and is designed to function as an independent agency. AJL is chaired by the Municipal Commissioner, and the local government keeps a vigilant check on the planning, construction and operations of the system. It coordinates with the various departments and agencies involved. It has three divisions under the General Manager, each headed by a Deputy General Manager. AJL takes full ownership of the BRT corridors, while adopting a PPP model for the functioning of nine of the system components. These include bus operations, fare collection, bus procurement, Intelligent Transport

System, park and pay, station cleaning, corridor facilities, maintenance, and leasing advertising.

Financial Resources and Management: The BRTS project was funded jointly by the national government, the state government and the local body. As part of the JnNURM funding pattern, the Ministry of Urban Development, Government of India, contributes 35 per cent of the total cost of the project. Another 15 per cent of the cost is borne by the Government of Gujarat. The balance 50 per cent is to be borne by the local government (AMC). The estimated cost for Phases 1 and 2 of the BRT system was INR 984 crore.The actual cost rendered after completion of the project was INR 1048 crore.

The Janmarg obtains its revenue from daily fare collections, selling advertisement rights along its corridors, and on-street parking. In 2011, the revenue of Janmarg matched its operational costs. As the next step of revenue generation, the sale of FSI along BRT corridors as part of the land use-transport integration concept has been initiated. An FSI increase of 25 per cent from the existing 1.8 to 2.35 on all roads with RoW greater than 30 m was proposed in the BRT Phase 2 report. Also, a further relaxation of 0.45 to the existing FSI of 2.8 is proposed, with payment of a fee, along corridors with RoW greater than 36 m (AMC, 2008).

Further, the Janmarg Board decided to differentiate the fares of AMTS and BRTS, with the BRTS fare being higher by 25 per cent. This, it appears, has led to increased competition between the two rather than making them collaborators. The BRTS is not very popular amongst the lower income groups. The higher fares of the BRTS compared to that of the AMTS (municipal) bus may be one reason, besides the coverage of the system (Mahadevia, Joshi, & Datey, 2013: 12).

3.3.2 *Resistance and its Management during Project Development*

In addition to strategies targeted towards broad groups such as public representatives, communities living across the city, personal vehicle users, abutting land users, parking etc., there were certain interferences from specific groups which were getting directly affected, and which needed to be managed. Though the list is long, this research presents three select cases of this type.

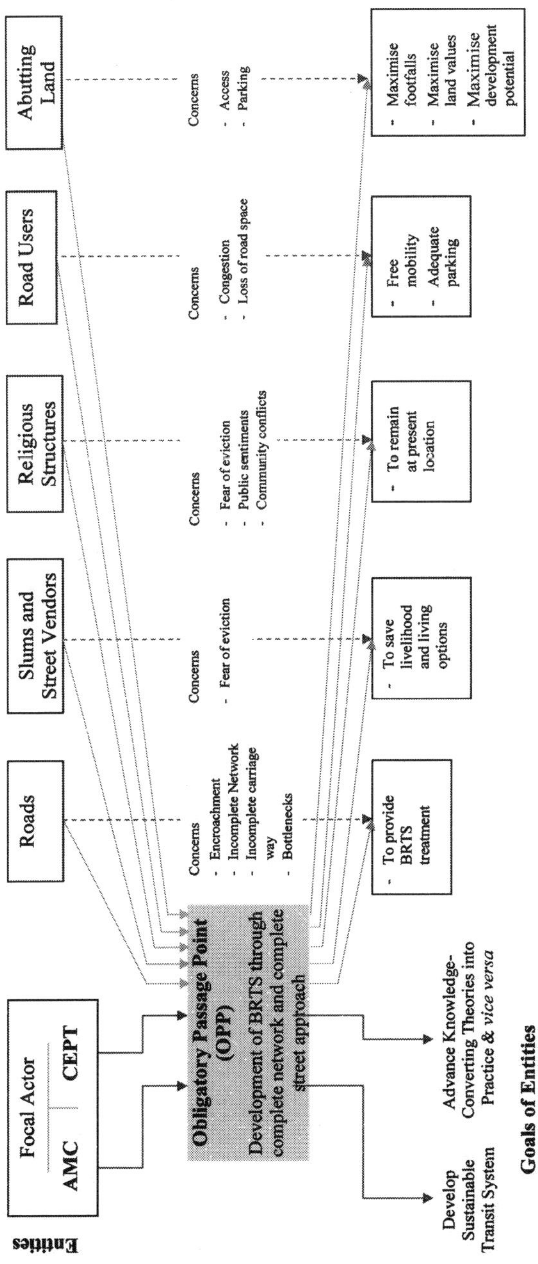

Fig. 3.7: Elements of Translation—Widening the Scope to Minimise the Resistance, 2007 to 2009

Figure 3.7 depicts the process wherein a simultaneous network is coming into existence towards producing BRTS. Some actors are different from the network discussed earlier and so are their interests. The OPP is also defined differently. At the end of this section, the mediating role played by judicial courts towards project development has been presented.

Case 1: Aligning Vadaj-Dudheshwar Bridge

The Ahmedabad Municipal Corporation (AMC) took up a new stretch from Vadaj to Dudheshwar (V-D) to relieve the Vadaj Circle from undue congestion. The construction of the V-D Bridge (now called Dhadhichi Bridge) also required construction of approach roads to the V-D Bridge on both sides, i.e. on the Vadaj side and the Dudheshwar side. Although the conceptualisation of the project started in 2006, its completion proved to be very difficult due to large-scale encroachments by residential and religious structures on both the approaches to the bridge.

Some of the project-affected families were successfully shifted to residential units constructed under the JnNURM scheme by the AMC. However, other families, most of them residing in the chawls of temple lands, did not want to relinquish their houses.

There were some popular religious structures such as temples, namely Kashmira Mahadev, Nilkanth Mahadev and Dudhnath Mahadev and Samadhis (tombs and cremation sites) and Deries (small shrines) on the path of the Vadaj and Dudheshwar approaches. The construction work could not be carried out due to resistance from these existing structures.

The two critical actors interfering in the project were the affected families (residing in the temple land located in the line of alignment of the bridge) and devotees and trustees of temples and other religious structures located in the path of the bridge alignment. The affected families were in dispute with the Municipal Corporation as they were living on a rental basis on the premises of the temple. A public interest litigation was filed, thus bringing in the Court as the third and mediating actor.

In response to the demolition notice, a few devotees and the trustees of Nilkanth Mahadev Temple, known as Dasnami Swatantra Niranjan Akhada, filed a Public Interest Litigation (PIL) Sp. Civil Application (SCA) No. 7558/2009 in the High Court of Gujarat in

Ahmedabad requesting that the Ahmedabad Municipal Corporation be restrained from demolishing, destroying, acquiring or in any manner altering the area comprising a temple (popularly known as Kashmira Mahadev of Vadaj) and an adjoining Samadhi. A further request was made to the Archaeological Survey of India (2nd respondent) to take control of the temple as it was considered an ancient monument of around 150 years, under Section 4 of the Ancient Monuments and Archaeological Sites and Remains Act, 1958. The PIL alleged that the AMC had decided to construct the bridge over the Sabarmati River, which could be constructed only by demolishing or altering the Kashmira Mahadev Temple.

In pursuance to the PIL, the Honourable High Court of Gujarat directed the Ahmedabad Municipal Corporation (1st Respondent) to consider alternatives so as not to demolish the Samadhi and the Shiv Temple. In response, AMC through its Engineering Department replied with two alternatives on 10 February, 2010. The alternatives suggested were:

Alternative 1 — In order to protect the Mahadev Temple and the Samadhi, which are on the Vadaj approach of the V-D Bridge, the AMC would enhance the distance between the pillars to save the temple, but the upper portion of construction of the Deries of the Samadhi would have to be done away with.

Alternative 2—As part of this alternative, the AMC would shift the approach so as to save the temple and even the upper portion of the Samadhi. Only the very top of the Samadhi would be affected because of the approach road, but the Samadhi, as such, would remain intact.

Although Alternative 2 was dearer by Rs. 6 crore than Alternative 1, the AMC expressed willingness to adopt any of the two alternatives suggested by the Honourable High Court. The counsel appearing on behalf of the petitioner stated that the petitioner would opt for Alternative 2. The High Court of Gujarat, taking into consideration the affidavits, ordered the adoption of Alternative 1 as it would serve the interest of all the parties and, in addition, would save the public exchequer of Rs. 6 crore.

In response to the implementation of the order of the Honourable High Court of Gujarat, the Dasnami Swatantra Niranjan Akhada Trust of Nilkanth Mahadev Mandir wrote a letter to the Municipal Commissioner, AMC. The letter stated that Alternative 1 was not exhaustively explained and described in the affidavit. Contrary to the statement that 'only the upper portion of construction of deries of Samadhi will go,' it was observed that not only a substantial portion of the upper part of the Samadhi was needed to be removed but it was further shockingly even the main gate of the temple was sought to be removed. The letter further emphasised resolution of the matter based on mutual understanding and mutual cooperation so that the religious sentiments inspired confidence and that no unpleasantness remained on either side.

As the former Deputy Commissioner (AMC) notes, intense negotiations subsequently took place between the AMC (especially the Engineering Department and the Estate Development Department) and Dasnami Swatantra Niranjan Akhada Trust, and finally, the construction of the steel girder was carried out in such a manner that the Kashmira Mahadev Temple and the Samadhi could be saved. The construction project got completed, and despite time and cost overruns, all the parties were satisfied with the solution. The affected hutment dwellers were also rehabilitated in houses built by the AMC under the JnNURM (Padia, 2014).

Case 2: Shifting of Huts from BRTS Route in Behrampura

The Bus Rapid Transit System project in the city of Ahmedabad provides for a 120 ft-wide road for the South Zone Behrampura ward. However, between the Vasna-Pirana overbridge and the Danilimda Police Chowki, several encroachments left only 15 feet to be used as a road while the rest of the road width had as many as 222 hutments. Another 177 hutments encroached the land near the Bridge and 320 hutment dwellers encroached the road called 'Mahakalinu Chapra.'

As the Deputy Commissioner explained, the construction of the 120 ft road required removal of the 320 hutments that were encroaching on the Mahakali Junction. The affected families filed a Special Civil Application in 2005 through the Jan Sangharsh Manch. The AMC represented itself before the Division Bench headed by the Honourable Chief Justice of Gujarat with a promise to provide alternative land under the JnNURM housing scheme. The petitions were disposed of with an order dated 16 April, 2007. The order provided that those who were evicted would be provided residential units under the JnNURM scheme. It also ordered that AMC should make arrangements to provide, according to its promise, 15 × 10 feet of space to every hutment unit at Piplaj till the time the housing under the JnNURM scheme was completed. The slum dwellers and the representatives of Jan Sangharsh Manch had several rounds of discussion with AMC officials before shifting from the site (Patel, 2013).

Subsequently, other similar challenges and resolutions occurred, first at Khodiyar Nagar Bridge (comprising 177 hutments) and then on the stretch from Khodiyar Nagar Bridge to Danilimda Police Chowki (comprising 222 hutments). The AMC resettled the affected families by providing them alternative housing facilities in order to be able to construct the 120 ft road.

The thousands of hutments, which faced the threat of displacement, along with their supporting organisations such as Jan Sangharsh Manch, advocates, AMC officials, Janmarg officials and the Honourable Court played a major role in resolving problems through negations and with court intervention wherever necessary. Here again, the role of the Court gets highlighted in the translation process.

Case 3: Peer Khamar Dargah

Peer Khamar Dargah was located on the main road connecting Danilimda with Maninagar, Kankaria and Isanpur. The structure was in the middle of an 80 ft wide road where only 30 ft were being used as navigable road, while the rest was under the possession of the dargah, the residence of the Moulvi and a small mosque. After completion of Dr. Baba Saheb Ambedkar Bridge near Pirana, the areas of Danilimda and the Paldi-Vasna area of western Ahmedabad became connected. But because of the bottleneck near the Dargah, most people coming from Isanpur, Maninagar and Kankaria had to use other roads or take the Sardar Patel Bridge at Paldi for going to the western side of the city.

After completion of the Baba Saheb Ambedkar Bridge at Pirana in 2007, the volume of traffic increased tremendously, and therefore, it became necessary to resolve this issue amicably. Besides being a road block to the building of the BRTS corridor to connect Maninagar and Kankaria to the system, the Peer Kamar Dargah was also an impediment to the laying of a storm water line. While the Dargah was old, the mosque and the residence of the Moulvi were built only a few years back by blocking more than half the road. As demolishing these structures was a very sensitive issue and was likely to lead to religious conflicts and law and order problems, the civic authorities took a conscious decision to resolve it through community involvement and negotiations with all stakeholders.

Negotiation with community leaders had already started in 2007 when the laying of drainage pipes in Maninagar ran into a problem. A storm water line from both the sides was constructed but it was not possible to connect them due to this religious structure midway. As the local community did not agree to shift the dargah or the house of the Moulvi, it was decided to stop the construction and start negotiations afresh.

A team was constituted under the leadership of the Special City Engineer of the Municipal Corporation in charge of water supply and drainage system. The Additional City Engineer (BRTS) and a few Additional City Engineers who worked there and were known to the community were also asked to join the team. The first level of negotiations with local community leaders, including the main Moulvi of the Peer Khamar Dargah, was started again in early 2008.

Another committee headed by the Deputy Municipal Commissioner was also constituted to negotiate with the elected representatives such as the local MLA, former municipal councillors of the area and MLAs and other elected representatives of the community.

The Municipal Commissioner also had several rounds of meetings with influential leaders of the community, office bearers, MLAs, and with influential religious leaders, such as the Imam, who had a final say in the resolution of such matters. They were requested to intervene for an amicable solution.

After four to five rounds of discussions, the seven-month-long negotiations yielded results. The local community finally agreed to give some way for the development of the BRTS as well as of the drainage line. And the Moulvi's residence, which lay between the Dargah and the mosque but was not a part of the religious structure, was removed with the consent of the local religious leaders to make enough space for two-way traffic on the road, keeping the Dargah in the middle. However, an exclusive BRTS corridor could not be made in this 75 metre long stretch (Patel, 2013).

There were several cases of religious structures coming in the way of the BRTS corridor. However, very few of them were impediments in the development of the BRTS. The two cases presented here are examples of successful translation.

3.3.2.1 *Mobilisation*

The tactics and mechanisms developed and utilised by the focal actors appear to have yielded positive results. By the beginning of 2009, the system was almost ready for opening commercial operations. The system needed to be tested. The focal actors decided to start bus operations on a trial basis in the first week of July 2009. Within a week, given the enthusiasm of the people, the trials became full-service operations; however, no fare was charged. These full service operations continued for three months.

The response to the three month long trial gave confidence to the focal actors to open the Janmarg, which saw continuous expansion and growth over the next four years. The network was expanded in quick succession, which gave an opportunity to convert each addition to a celebration. With every increase in the network and operational fleet, came more passengers to ride the BRTS. The AMTS withdrew its operations on BRT routes as and when BRTS started its operations. In 2011, with 45 km of operational network, the BRTS attracted as many as 1.35 lakh passengers on a normal working day. With a fleet of 67, this could be called by far the best operating efficiency in any bus system. The newspapers were full of reviews about how the BRTS had become a popular mode of travel. National and international recognition came aplenty.[6] City delegations, national and international, started visiting Ahmedabad. This goes to show that the focal actors had been successful in putting BRTS outside contestation, i.e. AMC-CEPT had successfully mobilised the BRTS in Ahmedabad. For all practical purposes, the design of Ahmedabad BRTS had been 'black-boxed'.

However, the situation changed after 2011. Although the network expanded, ridership did not grow. Collaborators once again started competing. Things again became fluid, and some, though not all, of the black-boxes got reopened. Stagnation in the ridership of Janmarg despite the increase in the network since 2011 was an indication that the network was getting destabilised.

3.3.3 *Dissidence: Betrayals and Controversies*

With the metro and regular buses being a part of the BRTS development strategy, the focal actors had taken the path of resistance and had

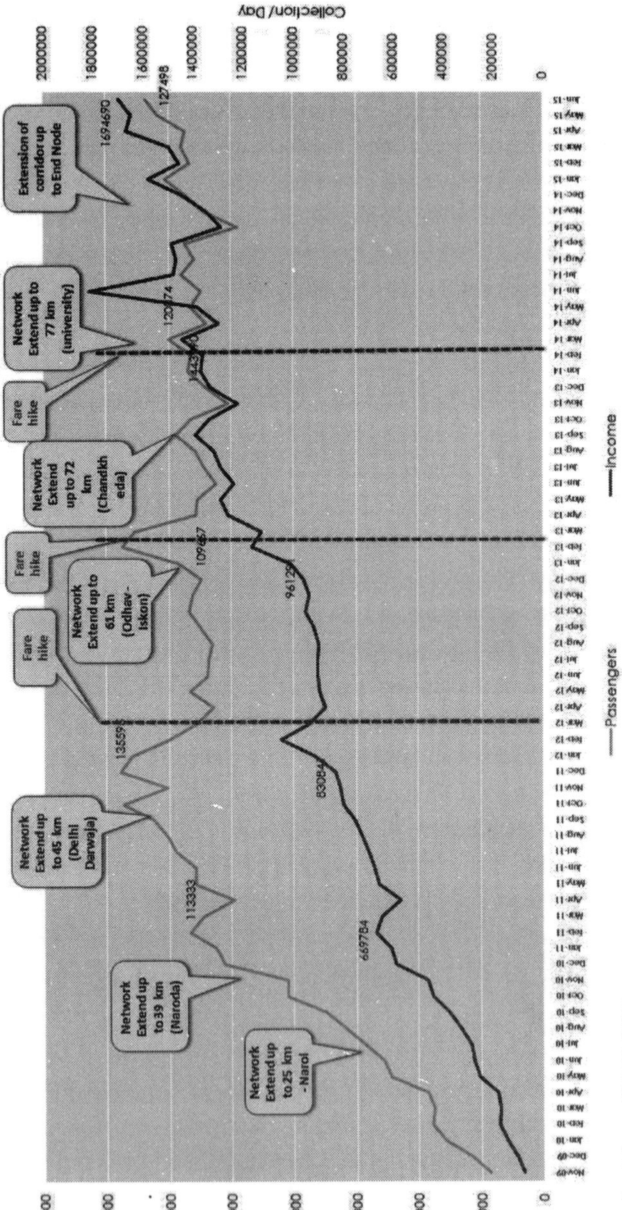

Source: Jan Marg, CEPT, 2015.

Fig. 3.8: BRTS Month-wise Average Daily Passengers, Fare-Revenue and Network Extension

succeeded in mobilising alliances with relevant stakeholders and thereby overcoming competition. In spite of such accommodative approach, three sets of dissidences emerged. The first came from the metro rail, the second from the monuments and roads, and finally, from the AMTS. This appears to be emerging out of their changing context/ issues and thereby changing interests as presented in Figure 3.9.

Each of these has been discussed briefly below.

3.3.3.1 *Metro Dissidence*

A company, Metro Gandhinagar-Ahmedabad (MEGA), was established in 2010 with the objective of implementing the metro system on a priority basis. This aim appears to have stemmed from the fact that many cities smaller than Ahmedabad in terms of population had gone ahead and started building metro systems. 'Metros are not a solution by themselves in any city. Metros are part of the transport system, and should be targeted for the very high demand corridors, above 50,000 passengers per hour per direction, because their cost is very high (Rs. 250–500 crore/km). For all other corridors (below 50,000 passengers per hour per direction), it is possible to handle the traffic operations with buses if the full BRT concepts are applied integrally' (Hidalgo as cited in Chandran, 2010). While the network was selected such that minimal overlap existed between the two systems, two sets of conflicts, if not resolved, would have had a serious impact on the functioning of BRTS.

For cost-saving reasons, MEGA decided to keep ground clearance at 5.5 metres while building an elevated viaduct. As the proposed rail overbridge of the two systems was crossing at Ashram Road, the Metro would have to go above this level, which meant a clearance of 12-13 metres. Objecting to take the viaduct at that level, MEGA wrote to AMC on 12 August, 2011 stating that the BRTS rail overbridge should go on the top as the metro would only go with a 5.5 metre clearance (Padia, Gujarat College RoB, 2013). The letter also stated that metros everywhere take precedence over all other projects. But technically, the BRTS bridge cannot be built with a clearance of 13 metres under any condition. Finally, it was resolved, with the Municipal Commissioner taking a very clear stand, that the RoB would be kept as designed by BRTS because it had been planned and tendered before the metro design finalisation. MEGA had to concede to this argument, but this impasse caused significant delay in the implementation of the

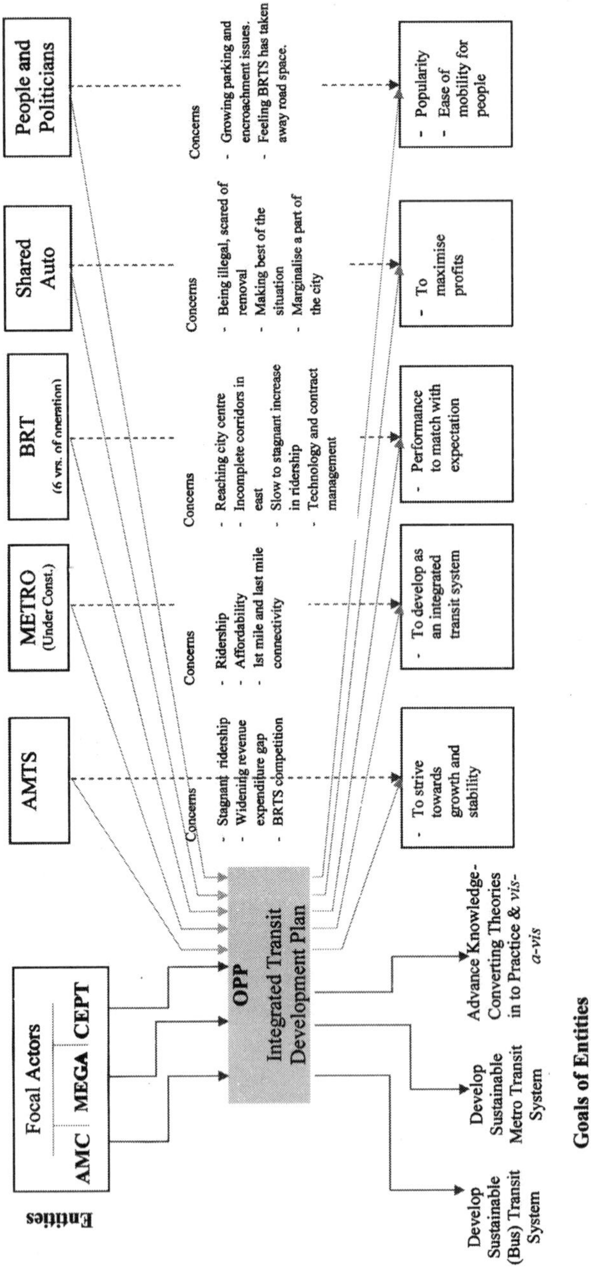

Fig. 3.9: Elements of Translation—Changing Concerns Leading to Dissidence, 2015

BRTS project. This delay created problems in operations in the city centre. Although one side of the network towards the city centre was complete, without completion of the bridge, the entire corridor had to be kept closed for many months. This was one event that destabilised the network formation.

However, with the resolution of this matter, it appeared as though all the issues between two types of systems had been resolved. This was, however, not to be. MEGA decided to relook at the corridors selected by DMRC, and came up with a network that looked like a mirror image of the BRTS network. The corridors were running parallel to the BRTS network in most parts. This would have made both BRTS and the Metro systems unviable (Paul, 2012). Despite this, a DPR for metro was prepared in 2012 and design work was also taken up on many sections of the network. However, AMC was successful in thwarting the metro alignment in parallel to BRTS by successfully canvasing with the state government.

3.3.3.2 *Dissidence from Monuments and Streets*

AMC, as per the plan, started to expand its network into the inner areas of the city. There were delays in building the aforementioned rail overbridge. Besides, the plan for building an elevated corridor in the congested core area had to be dropped due to changes in the rules at the national level. The Ancient Monuments Act was amended in 2010 which banned any construction within 100 metres of a declared monument. Ahmedabad is a 600-year-old city with several historical monuments in the old part of the city. Besides, in some areas while the corridor was segregated, bus stations had not been built owing to litigation. As a result, the expansion of the BRTS network was slow and discontinuous. With a major portion (82 km) of the network having been built, AJL expanded its services to the city centre. It had to cover some parts in mixed traffic as the corridor could not be built. This diluted the concept of BRTS in a significant manner.

3.3.3.3 *Dissidence from AMTS*

Although AMTS had been restocked with new buses and AMC extended its financial support, the rise in ridership was observed only in the initial period. Post-2011, the system started to experience a stagnant, even declining ridership once again. While on the one hand, BRTS was getting applauded nationally and internationally, the AMTS faced severe criticism.

The problems of excessive manpower, labour absenteeism, liabilities arising out of the implementation of the Pay Commission recommendations, growing social welfare benefits to employees continued to persist, widening AMTS's revenue-expenditure gap. Given this background, AMTS saw in AJL a competitor rather than a collaborator.

The creation of AJL was itself an issue. Given that the AMTS has been in existence for five decades, it would seem logical to assign the responsibility of the BRTS to the AMTS. Revamping the AMTS was also seen as an option. However, given the number of complications such as pending court cases and manpower issues, it was concluded that handing the responsibility of BRTS to AMTS would jeopardise the interest of the newly developed system. Hence, project planners had decided to create a special purpose vehicle, a company under the Companies Act, to manage Janmarg Ahmedabad BRTS. Accordingly, the Ahmedabad Janmarg Ltd. was registered in 2008. In creating a separate organisation, the AMC attempted to insulate and protect the new system from the liabilities and poor professional culture of the existing organisation, an obvious move to mitigate risk. Both organisations belonged to the AMC. The AMTS was dependant on the AMC for funds to meet its operational losses. Hence, it was believed that the AMTS would not object. Going further, the project planners had attempted to cajole AMTS through a series measures which included:

- Inclusion of all relevant stakeholders on the AJL board.
- AJL procured 550 new buses under JnNURM and leased them at INR 1 to AMTS.
- Senior AMC Deputy Commissioner was given charge of AJL as its Executive Director.
- All senior functionaries were brought from AMC on deputation.
- AJL as well as AMC had resolved that as and when the AJL network expanded, AMTS would withdraw its services from the BRTS network and redeploy those to serve the under-serviced areas.

This arrangement worked well in the initial phase of BRTS expansion. To avoid overlaps, the AMTS either withdrew its services through route alteration or at least reduced its frequency. The AJL increased its network incrementally, starting with 12.5 km. With every increase in the network, ridership increased more than proportionately. In 2012, with 45 km of BRTS network, AJL serviced an average of 1.35 lakh passengers a day and fully recovered its operating costs. The popularity of AJL was at its peak, with its monthly customer rating remaining high at 8.5+ on a 10-point scale. With this achievement, the AMC's objective of operating the bus system seemed to have been attained, albeit partly (only through AJL). The interests of the AMTS had been translated to align with AJL's interests, i.e. city interests.

While the services of AJL expanded to the inner core, AMTS continued its operations in these areas. The latter's bus frequency was very high as routes from different parts came to the city centre. As a result, a new precarious situation emerged. On the BRTS network (82 km), AJL supplied about 35,000 bus km a day. On this network, the supply of AMTS was 45,000 km! In the remaining 610 km of road network, AMTS supply was 1,15,000 km.

Table 3.2: Transit Supply in Ahmedabad

Item	AMTS	AJL
Total Bus Route road network (km)	610	
Transit supply (bus km) – rounded	190,000	
Bus km/km road	310	
BRTS network (km)	82 km (Except for 6 km, on which both services operate)	
Transit Supply (bus km) – rounded on BRT network	45,000	35,000

Source: CoE-UT, 2013.

From the above, it is evident that transit supply in the city is skewed and there is an oversupply in certain parts of the network whereas the services are thinly spread over a large part of the network. The AMTS was competing with the BRTS with the same buses which the AJL had provided to the AMTS. With new and better quality buses and a fare advantage, AMTS started giving increased competition. The ridership of BRTS stagnated despite an increase in the network length. Surprisingly, even AMTS ridership decreased from 800,000 a day to 500,000 a day! In an effort to build an efficient organisation, (which seemed to have been achieved), the very system that seemed to have been stabilised, was now under threat. With the key decision makers being the same, it was assumed that they would side with more efficient and customer-friendly operations and the new innovation would get stabilised. In addition, AMC's financial control over AMTS and providing the new buses were thought to be adequate measures to translate their interest in favour of more efficient operations.

With the persuasion of AMC, the AMTS attempted a route rationalisation. While CEPT had suggested a gradual stage-wise process, the AMTS, however, decided to do the process in one go. Without any advance public information, the AMTS stopped services, not just on the BRTS network but on the entire city network! This led to a chaotic situation with AMTS's own employees descending on the streets! In fact, a day before the stoppage of services, the AMTS had issued thousands of student concession passes for the same routes which they had decided to discontinue! This raised doubts about AMTS's commitment to the plan.

Route rationalisation is of paramount importance in any efficient urban transport. Once the Metro came in, it should have led to further route rationalisation between AMTS, BRTS and Metro. AMTS should have fed BRTS and the Metro and BRTS should have been a parallel system comparable to the Metro and also act as a feeder to the Metro on certain routes. This work should have been left to the experts with the involvement of stakeholders and there should not have been any needless competition amongst the three, since all three modes were funded by the Government and also subsidised. The route rationalisation could not be done effectively because of inherent opposition from the AMTS lobby. It was deliberately timed in such a manner that it created public unrest and hence the idea was put on the backburner (Mohapatra, 2015).

3.3.4 *(Re) Translation*

Two important developments appear to be enabling a set of transformation processes in the actor-network. The MEGA organisational structure was restructured in 2013. The Government decided to take a relook at the entire Metro planning in Ahmedabad. DMRC was once again asked to prepare a DPR on demand estimation with CEPT support. DMRC, in its revised report, adopted the original network of 2005 with some modifications. The modifications included shifting of the north-south alignment from Ashram Road to the existing metre-gauge railway line and extension of the east-west corridor beyond Central Railway station towards the eastern periphery. The network in the centre of the city was to be built as an underground system. In this new scheme of things, integration with the BRTS as well as with other systems was explicitly planned. Last mile connectivity was taken into consideration in a complete manner. Last mile connectivity, which includes integration of various transit modes as well as local accessibility, had been made conditional in approving the DPR (MEGA DPR, 2013). With this, along with the AMC, MEGA is likely to become a focal actor in the times ahead.

AMC has recently decided to allow AMTS buses (called AMTS-BRTS) on select BRTS corridors. At present there are 46 such buses that ply on the BRTS corridor. The city is also putting in place a common city payment system. As part of this, fare integration, both of AMTS and BRTS, and also of the Metro, as and when it is ready, has been envisaged.

3.4 Discussion and Summary

Urban transport, being a multi-dimensional activity, requires multiple actors to take the lead to problematise and make efforts to create a stable network. In Ahmedabad, inadequacies in urban transport were identified as a critical problem, and towards this end, the state government (GIDB, UDD, Transport and PWD departments), local government, development authority, traffic police and MEGA (subsequently) all have a stake. Each one of them, with their respective versions of problematisation, has initiated action. Each of them is an actor network by itself, and mobilising them all as a larger network is a major effort in this initiative.

The discussion in the chapter outlines that, in the process of project development, stabilisation is not a static state. During the life cycle of a project, stabilisation and destabilisation occur constantly, and the focal actors need to constantly attempt to mobilise and remobilise associations to keep the project in a stable state. Although project formulation needs to be done in great detail, if flexibility is not built into it, the success of the project could be at stake. Hence, the development of large projects in the public arena entail continuously evolving innovations.

While the development of BRTS involves much negotiation, in the process of attempting to translate the interests of other actors, the focal actors may eventually compromise their own interest.

The metro system is often taken for granted, and, to put it in ANT terminology, it is black-boxed. While the BRTS has spread rapidly in cities across the world (especially in Latin America and China), its adoption in other parts of the world is riddled with controversy. While the city of Ahmedabad has increased its network at a rapid pace and black-boxed it, it appears that some black-boxes have been reopened.

NOTES

1. Ahmedabad Agglomeration accounts for 78 per cent of the total population of the district (AMC, 2006).
2. To capture the inadequately serviced transit market, an alternative system in the form of 'shared auto-rickshaws' emerged as informal public transit service suppliers. They used three-wheeled vehicles (auto-rickshaws) with designed/approved carrying capacity of three, plus the driver. They are supposed to provide 'intermediary public transit service' which has the following four conditions regulated through a permit. The permit conditions are: (1) they will not have fixed routes, (2) they will not have fixed schedules, (3) the fare will be fixed and pre-decided and chargeable on the basis of kilometre run, and not on stop to stop, and (4) they are supposed to be accessible to all when not on hire, but once on hire, they would be accessible only to that user and no one else. Shared auto operators are found to violate all the above.
3. Share of shared auto.
4. This type of contract is known as gross-cost contract in which the fare risk is with the public authority and the operations risk is with the private operator.
5. GIDB letter, addressed to Director, CEPT University, 12 February, 2005.
6. The initial proposal was to develop 217 km of BRT network.
7. To accommodate two BRT lanes in the middle, two mixed traffic lanes on either side, medians and foot path of reasonable size, a street width of 30 metres is desirable.
8. BRTS, by 2011, had won the prestigious 'Prime Minister's Best Mass Transit Award', 'Sustainable Transport Award' and many more.

4
Artifacts, Programme of Action, Scripts and Inscriptions

4.1 Introduction

BRT is a system in which several elements are put together to function as one system to deliver a superior quality of service. 'Superior quality' here implies a service that is rapid, reliable, safe, secure, efficient, environmentally sustainable, financially affordable and high capacity. Provision of such a service is attempted through delegation of control to non-humans, i.e. to technological artifacts. These artifacts are designed such that they exert control over the operating environment in order to deliver a superior service. As noted by Latour, "artifacts can be deliberately designed to both replace human action and constrain and shape the actions of other humans" (Latour, 1992: 230). Further, "design activities, in varying degrees, ultimately aim to create, modify, enable and/or constrain some capacities of action through designed artifacts" (Kocabili, Gemainboeck, Saunders & Dong, 2011: 2).

This chapter attempts to describe the design of major artifacts that BRTS Ahmedabad planners designed and developed. While analysing the design of artifacts, ANT concepts, namely delegation, scripts, inscription, programme of action, irreversibility and black-box, have been adopted. Though these concepts have been explained in Chapter 2, for the sake of clarity and continuity, they are briefly recapitulated below.

The word artefact, or artifact, is derived from the Latin word 'arte', — ablative of ars (art), and factum, the past participle of facere (to make) (Hilpinen, 2011: 2). According to Webster's

Third New International Dictionary, an artifact is 'a usually simple object (as a tool or an ornament) showing human workmanship and modification as distinguished from a natural object.' The Oxford English Dictionary defines an artifact (artefact) as 'anything made by human art and workmanship; an artificial product.' However, ANT uses the term in a much broader sense: 'An artifact may be defined as an object that has been intentionally made or produced for a certain purpose'(Hilpinen, 2011: 2).

Artifacts and tools are essential elements for mediating and supporting human 'what-ever-kind-of activities.' Artifacts are characterised as 'what-ever-kind of device' explicitly designed to embed some kind of functionality that can be properly used by humans to do their work (Ricci, 2006: 4). Artifacts can be deliberately designed to both replace human action and constrain and shape the actions of other humans (Latour, 1992: 151). The term 'design of artifacts,' (Akrich, Callon, & Latour, 2002) is used to mean inscribing a programme of action into technological artifacts. This, then, is a process of delegation of agency to non-humans, i.e. to artifacts. Inscription is the process whereby translations of one's interests are embodied into technical artifacts. Callon (1991) claims that any component of a heterogeneous network of skills, practices, artifacts, institutional arrangements, texts and contracts that create a social order might be the material for inscriptions cited in the Action Network Theory weblog (ANT and Inscriptions, 2015). The inscription includes programmes of action for the users, and it defines roles to be played by users and the system. "By inscribing programmes of actions into a piece of technology, the technology becomes an actor imposing its inscribed programme of action on its users. The inscribed patterns of use may not succeed because the actual use deviates from it" (Latour, 1991, as cited in Lawer, 2005: 102).

Programme of Action is a task with a certain goal given to an actant (Mattozzi: 12). Inscriptions may be strong or weak. Depending on the strength of the inscription, the users may follow the programme of action or they may disobey it, i.e. they may decide to follow an anti-programme of action. Whether the programme of action has been followed or not, will depend on irreversibility of the network. The process of inscription is cumulative, and to make the network stronger, multiple and repetitive inscriptions may be tried out.

Irreversibility and black-box are two ANT concepts that explain the stability and durability of the network. Irreversibility is the degree of resistance against the actor-network. Stronger inscriptions result in a higher degree of irreversibility and vice versa. It affects the possibility of the system reverting to its original position.

Black boxes are actor-networks in which many elements are made to act as one. A network is stated to be stabilised when it is black-boxed. This means people are no longer interested in knowing what the content and behaviour of the technological artifact is, but instead, the content and behaviour is accepted as common knowledge.

"An artifact's script is a rich and complex way of understanding both the motivations and domain specific assumptions of designers in the design process, as well as the way in which real-users interact with the affordances expressed through the internal agency of the technical object/artifact" (Akrich, M., 1992, as cited in Carey, 2013: 2).

Callon (1991) identifies four aspects of the notion of inscription as cited in (ANT and Inscriptions, 2015):

- What is inscribed (The designer writes the script with an anticipation of use).
- Who inscribes (Actor-Designer, User).
- How they are inscribed (what material form).
- How powerful are the inscriptions (what it takes to go against an inscription).

With the above as its conceptual basis, this chapter explores the design, development and operations of key artifacts of the Ahmedabad BRTS. While there is a long list of artifacts designed as part of the BRTS, this work focuses on three key artifacts — the street network, the stations (and the elements within it), and the bus (and its elements). Other related artifacts such as the fare collection system (policy, structure, collection system and equipment), passenger information systems, operating plan and procedures, governance mechanisms etc. are critical and are considered wherever relevant.

This chapter is divided into six parts. Following the introduction (Section 1) above, section 2 describes the pre-project context. This is followed by the programme of action and the scripts, which the designers of Ahmedabad BRT evolved and inscribed into artifacts to create a conducive environment for BRT operations (Section 3, 4 and

5). Section 6 discusses and draws conclusions about the inscription and the attempts to ensure network durability.

4.2 Pre-(BRT) Project Context

According to the detailed project report (AMC, 2006), the number of registered vehicles was increasing at a rapid rate. The composition of vehicle stock was not balanced. Some of the mobility issues highlighted by the study were as follows:

- Urban sprawl, jobs going beyond the municipal limits, and decline in population within the old city were some of the factors influencing transit demand.
- About two-thirds of the vehicles[1] were two wheelers (AMC, 2006). Fitted with 2-stroke engines, these were not only considered to be the prime contributors to the deteriorating air quality but were also responsible for disorganised and haphazard mobility. Because of their undisciplined movement on roads, the two wheelers were a major traffic hazard.
- Auto-rickshaws were the other group that caused concern due to their major contribution to increasing pollution. They were known to be using adulterated fuel, which was harmful for human health. Their road-use pattern, too, was undisciplined. They would park on the street, disregarding parking regulations, and driving on the wrong side of the road was the norm rather than an exception. Through their clandestine operations as informal transit providers, auto-rickshaws threatened the sustainability of public transit development.
- Ahmedabad was declared the fourth most polluted city in the country with regard to air quality. As noted in the DPR (AMC, 2006: 4-10), "the poor enforcement in controlling the IPT modes of three-wheelers and allowing them to operate virtually as stage carriage vehicles in contravention of legal provisions ... has eroded ... revenue of AMTS leading to deterioration of AMTS."
- The growing number of cars, and the haphazard parking of cars along the road, constricted road space, resulting in traffic jams.
- The municipal transport was on the decline.

- Facilities for bicycles, such as cycle paths, did not exist, and footpaths were lacking both in terms of coverage and quality.

On the supply side, there were severe limitations.

- In terms of the road network, the total area under roads within the jurisdiction of Ahmedabad Municipal Corporation was 1272 km, or 7.5 per cent (as opposed to the desired level of 15-18 per cent). Considering the travel demand, a network of 155 km was identified for developing the BRTS, of which, 58 km was to be implemented in the first phase (AMC, 2006: 7-13). Subsequently, another 30 km of street network was included as BRTS phase-2 extension.
- The Right of Way (RoW) of the network selected for BRTS development had varying widths (60 m, 40 m, 30 m, 24 m and 18 m). At many places on the ground, however, the RoW actually measured much less than what was found in the records. Further, the developed carriageway on these streets was about a third to a half of the available RoW.

The impact of the rapid growth in transport demand and its inadequate supply had resulted in significant transport problems (AMC, 2006). Some of these problems are listed below:

- V/C ratio on the critical part of the network was close to '1'.
- Network speed on major roads was about 14-16 kmph.
- Increasing road accidents, most of which were concentrated on major roads.
- High pedestrian and bicyclist deaths due to the lack of appropriate infrastructure.
- Transport vehicles accounted for 60 to 70 per cent of the total pollution load of the city.
- The SPM and RSP levels were found to be consistently higher than the National Ambient Air Quality Standards.
- Deterioration of transit services threatened the long-term sustainability of the existing public transport in the city.

This was the context that led to initiation of the development of BRTS in Ahmedabad.

4.3 The Design: Programme of Action, Scripts and Inscription

The Detailed Project Report, while summarising the challenges and opportunities, expressed the intent behind the development of the BRTS. Referring to the declining bus ridership and the increasing role of auto-rickshaws as informal transit operators (which are illegal and unsafe) as a major challenge, it underscored the need for a strategic intervention rather than another 'gap filling' exercise — an intervention that would not only recover the ridership lost to auto-rickshaws but would also 'bid for a larger share of travel demand.' This, the report notes, 'can only be possible with adequate, affordable, convenient, quality public transit service' (AMC, 2006: 6-1). The essence of the argument was that the new mode to be introduced had to be significantly different and superior (both qualitatively and quantitatively) to the existing bus service run by the AMTS. These became the defining characteristic features for the new system design, i.e. the script for the designer.

The system to be designed was expected to fulfil several objectives concerning the users, the operators and the society. Rapid mobility, reliability, affordability, convenience, safety and security were some of the features desired by the users. Efficiency, financial sustainability and durability were the factors that concerned the operators. In addition to the overall system efficiency at the city level, minimising polluting emissions with a view to minimising negative externalities was the main concern of the society as a whole.

Based on the above concerns, the programme of action, as envisaged by the designers, involved —

- The creation of the 'mobility system' itself (with in the desired capabilities), and
- Control of the environment within which the mobility systems had to operate.

A parallel may be drawn with the navigational context described by Law (2010: 1) in 'On the Methods of Long Distance Control: Vessels, Navigation, and the Portuguese Route to India.' The narration is about Portuguese expansion and the construction of the navigational context undertaken by the Portuguese in order to secure global mobility and the durability of their vessels. It also suggested that "the three classes of emissaries — documents, devices and drilled people — have, together and separately, been particularly important for long distance control, and that the dominance of the West since the sixteenth century may be partly explained in terms of crucial innovations in the methods by which passive agents of these three types are produced and interrelated" (Law, 2010: 2).

On similar lines, the success of the development and operations of the BRTS in Ahmedabad largely relates to the way the artifacts listed here were designed.

The main artifacts (non-human actors) of the BRTS include:

- Streets
- Stations
- Buses
- Operations system

The attempt here is to describe the design of the above artifacts in terms of the designers' motive/programme of action (anti-programme) and its inscription. Interface with users in terms of whether they adopted the programme of action or followed their own (anti) programme is also discussed.

4.4 Designing the BRT Street

As stated earlier, the existing road configuration and predominance of two-wheelers, auto-rickshaws operating as informal transit providers, increasing number of cars, mixed traffic modes, lack of lane discipline and jaywalking represented the common scene on the streets of Ahmedabad.

Making the bus a faster, safer, affordable, attractive, environmentally sustainable and an economically viable system for providing high capacity people movement, thus became the designers' programme of action.

Towards this end, the first artifact to be created was the exclusive bus lane.

4.4.1 *Exclusive lanes*

Ensuring '*rapidness*' of the BRT system on the roads of Ahmedabad where the infrastructure and user behaviour least supported the ease of movement of buses, was the biggest design challenge. A critical element that makes the BRT bus move rapidly is to give it exclusive passage, i.e. to segregate bus movement from that of other vehicles.

The practice of segregation of vehicles by their size and functionality is accepted universally as a way to minimise on-street conflict and to thereby improve safety and operations efficiency. The road transport vehicles come in different dimensions and exhibit different movement characteristics in terms of speed, acceleration, deceleration, turning radius etc. On roads with a high level of traffic, conflicts between vehicles may be created when heavy vehicles, fast-moving cars, auto-rickshaws and two-wheelers have to share the roadway with the less protected and slower vehicles such as bicycles, and with pedestrians. Segregation of heavy from light vehicles and fast from slow-moving vehicles would make mobility safer, smoother and more efficient. Creation of bus lanes on city streets is essentially an extension of this logic. The provision of exclusivity to bus lanes would not only facilitate faster movement of buses, but would also enable cars, auto-rickshaws and two-wheelers to move faster and more safely. However, this is not without controversy. In already developed areas, the streets and urban spaces are currently in use. Current users, by virtue of the fact that they have been using it (pre-project), tend to believe that they have ownership rights over the road space and would contest any alteration from its current position. To put it differently, BRTS, when developed as an urban insert, would involve reallocation of the already distributed 'use rights.' This would lead to a new set of controversies over space use, irrespective of the efficiency, legality or authorisation of the use. (Please note that streets are public spaces; they include the carriageway as well as the abutting foot path, access etc.).

In anticipation of resistance from current users and the current transit system, the designers of BRT adopted three sets of tactics (scripts) to minimise the resistance.

Network selection: The first tactic was that the network selected was the path of least resistance. This may be seen in three of the eight guiding principles adopted by the designers, which were followed in the case of network selection, and are as follows (AMC, 2006):

- Connect 93 busy places and avoid busy corridors.
- Add capacity to the network and draw part of the capacity for BRTS.
- Select that part of the network where it is feasible to insert the BRTS design.

Minimum street width requirement: In selection of the network, it was ensured that only the adequately wide parts of the network were selected for BRT development. To accommodate two BRT lanes plus a minimum of two mixed traffic lanes and a foot path on either side, 24 metres of street width was considered to be the minimum required to accommodate BRTS. Bus stations (3.5 to 4 metre wide) would have to be accommodated with minimum widening locally. In some cases, BRT had to be accommodated even in 22 m wide streets but with 5.5 to 6 m wide intermediary lanes for mixed traffic mobility. On streets with less than these widths, one way BRT was proposed. On wider streets, depending on the width available, bicycle lanes, a third mixed-traffic lane, and parking-cum-utility lanes were added in that order of priority.

Completion of network: Completion of the network through two river bridges and about 20 flyovers opened up new options for designers to select routes that were currently not in much use (Refer Figure 4.1). In addition, two small new links were added to the network. The above actions also added significant capacity to the network. Side-by-side, wherever possible, the Rights of Way (RoW) or Carriage Ways (CW), or both, were widened.

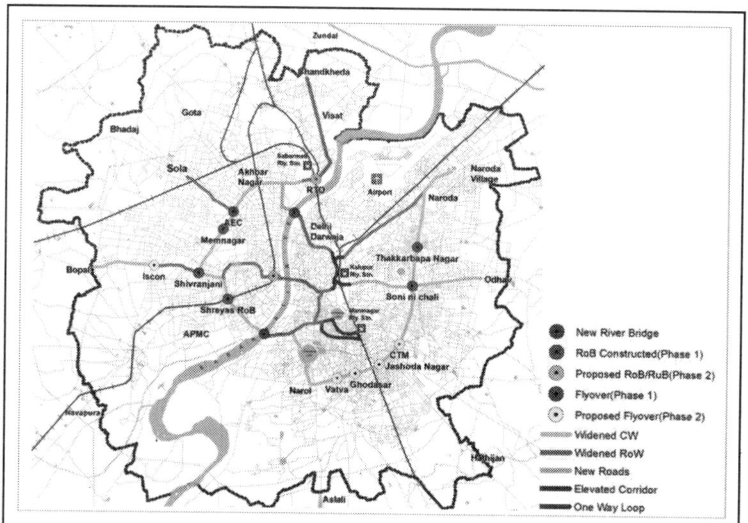

Fig. 4.1: Completion of network

Complete street design: Eighty per cent of the 88 km of the BRT network in Ahmedabad has been widened (RoW or CW, or both).

Fig. 4.2: Reallocation of space along BRT corridor — Before BRTS

Fig. 4.3: Reallocation of space along BRT corridor — After BRTS

Adopting a complete-street approach, the city developed full RoW including all elements of a street. Complete streets are those which focus on moving people and not vehicles by providing exclusive and defined spaces for public and private vehicular transport, walking, cycling and street activities.With this arrangement, the personalised vehicles in the mixed traffic lanes got back road space equal to what was available before the project. An added benefit was that the mixed traffic lanes did not have to accommodate buses. As a result, in the short and medium term, both the buses in the exclusive corridor and the personalised vehicles in the mixed traffic lanes benefited due to segregation (Refer Figure 4.2 and 4.3). Efficiency gains due to reduced conflict are significant (CoE-UT, CEPT University, 2013). However, in the long run, with high rates of motorisation continuing and vehicle composition changing in favour of cars (from that of two-wheelers), the capacity of the mixed traffic lanes will be exhausted.

Exclusive bus lanes: While anticipated resistance from those displaced (current users) was minimised through selection of the path of least resistance, because of the adoption of the complete street approach, the problem of undisciplined traffic behaviour remained to be addressed. Bus lane provision in the form of lane markings and signs, as is common in European and Southeast Asian cities, would not have worked in Ahmedabad. It is well known that Indians do not voluntarily follow traffic rules or signals unless the police physically enforce them on the streets. In this situation, the issue was whether the agency to enforce could be limited to weak artifacts such as traffic signals, sign boards, lane markings etc., or would it need to be strengthened by delegating enforcement to stronger non-human actors.

Protecting exclusivity: Towards protecting exclusivity of BRTS lanes, a series of artifacts (detailed below) have been designed based on the assessment of the socio-economic conditions and behavioural patterns of the various users of the streets.

Median *vs.* curb side: The debate over placement of bus lanes in the median or on the curb side evinces a lot of interest amongst the general public as well as the professionals. This, despite the fact that, historically, transit systems (such as trams or present day LRT and BRT) are generally located in the centre of the carriage way, mainly to facilitate personalised traffic movement and turns. The perception of the common man is that the footpath is where people walk and that is the most accessible place from where buses should pick them up. Accordingly, placing bus lanes on the curb side is defended. However, curb-side lanes pose serious constraints in operations as the friction with road-side activities increases as one moves from the centre towards the side. An important aspect is that as most activities along the street have direct access from the street, the bus lane would have to be punctured every now and then to provide access to the side. Given our socio-economic conditions, managing parking and other encroachments, street vending etc., this does not appear feasible. A comparison of the side and middle lane designs is presented in Table 4.1. Considering the advantages of the median/central lane, Ahmedabad adopted the central lane model. In this model, instead of buses coming near the footpaths to pick up pedestrians, pedestrians walk to the bus stations in the centre of the road.

Table 4.1: Median lane *versus* Side lane design

Side Lane	Median Lane
Compatible with conventional bus door configuration on curb side (left side)	Easy to integrate bus flow with other flow at the intersection. Traditional bus-door configuration on left side of travel can be retained by providing bus stops on left side.
Easier accessibility from the pedestrian pathway	Pedestrians have to cross over to the median at pedestrian crossings.
Total road width occupied for bus lane is doubled	Optimum road width for movement in both directions.
Capacity remains underutilised	Infrastructure created can be utilised even if BRTS is withdrawn.
Cost intensive treatment at junctions would have to be carried out as free left turn for regular traffic would be cut off	Slight diversion to other traffic when a bulge is provided to accommodate the bus stops.
Examples: London, Singapore	*Examples*: Bogotá, Curitiba, Ahmedabad.

Source: AMC, 2006.

Soft *vs.* Hard Segregation: Segregation can be done by simple lane marking, by a single median, double medians, double median with 1-metre-high railing, and double median with 1-metre-high railing with thick shrubs. The designers went through a series of options before deciding on the final option — double median with 1-metre-high railing with thick shrubs.

As stated earlier, with low levels of compliance with traffic rules in the city, the simple lane-marking option was not adequate to prevent personalised vehicles from entering the bus lane. Although a single median would have been sufficient and economical, because of the clearly demarcated street edges, in many cases the street light poles had to be installed in the median. This called for a double median covering a width of 750 mm (although it varied with the width of the street), which was adequate to erect a street light pole. These poles were later also used as advertisement boards. Since people were used to jaywalking, which not only causes disruptions in the movement of traffic but also becomes a safety hazard, a 1 metre-high railing was installed on either side of the median. Although the railing prevented people from entering the BRT lane, it was still possible for the more enthusiastic to climb over it. Utilising the width available, the space along the railing was used for landscaping. Trees as well as shrubs were planted; the shrubs specifically to make crossing difficult.

Pedestrian crossings with prevention of jaywalking through medians and railings, pedestrian crossings were designed at every 250 metres (including at junctions), with provision for wheelchair facility, and controlled through signal systems.

Intersections and their management is important for three reasons — to facilitate turning movements, manage vehicle conflict and facilitate turnarounds for the BRTS (at Route Terminating Points).

With BRTS, operations management of junctions becomes difficult as the number of traffic signal phases multiply and they tend to grow longer than the acceptance level of users. With the choice of closed system of operations, it was possible to keep the junction management task simple by avoiding four-arm BRT movement. Ahmedabad has only one junction where BRTS moves on all four arms. Crossing at this junction has been designed at two levels, with bus stations at both the levels. There are three junctions with BRT running on three arms. These are treated either with a big roundabout or with traffic signals. These also facilitate route termination where required.

Having taken care of BRTS movement, the conflict between mixed traffic and BRT had to be minimised. The designers, as part of the original plan, had identified seven junctions where grade separated junctions were to be built. These were to be split flyovers keeping buses at grade so as to keep them accessible. As part of the plan, three split-flyovers and five flyovers were built across the BRTS corridor (AMC, 2006: Chapter 8).

An area traffic control system was designed to give priority to buses. In one signal phase, the BRTS got two green phases in a single cycle by aligning it with direct and right turning movements. Green time required for buses to cross the intersection is only 10 seconds.

Despite these artifacts designed to discourage/prevent entry into BRT lanes, it is still possible for vehicles to enter the lanes through the junctions. In addition to traffic signal control system, two other instruments have been put in place to prevent other vehicles from entering the corridor. The first is in the form of a notification by the Police Commissioner under the Police Act, Section 33(1)b. Under this provision, the traffic police have powers to impound vehicles other than BRTS buses which enter the corridor. A separate security arrangement was made for BRTS by recruiting ex-army personnel by the city traffic police.

4.5 Designing BRT Stations

A BRT station is not merely a piece of infrastructure designed and developed to provide passenger access to buses; it is the interface between the people and the transit system where they expect quality service. It is a place where passengers feel the need to be safe, and a place where they get to know how to reach different destinations in the city, and how much it would cost. For an operator, it is a point where he meets his customers and a point of revenue collection. For the station operator, it is a place where he earns his livelihood, and where he needs to deal with several hundreds of people everyday. For a driver, it is a place where he picks up people to ferry them safely to another station. For the society at large, it is a point where mass movements from many directions culminate into a controlled, regulated system; a meeting place; a quality urban space that provides an identity to the area and, more importantly, an image to the system.

BRTS designers in Ahmedabad had to materialise this idea where, until then, the concept of a bus station was that of a mere footpath with a waiting bench, sometimes with a roof over it and a sign board indicating its location, and where buses seldom docked at the designated bays. This section analyses the formation of the network — bus stations, from its conception to commencement. The focus is on its functional aspects and how artifacts were designed to achieve the required functionalities, i.e. to shape human behaviour. As described above, a bus station is an amalgam of several artifacts made to function as a system. This work focuses on the following functionalities.

- Bus station *per se* in terms of its location, spacing and capacity.
- Bus access for boarding and alighting control.
- Passenger access to stations, including access control systems (such as zebra crossings, signals, speed breakers, bollards).
- Ensuring universal access.
- Fare systems.
- Passenger information.
- There are also other functionalities, which are not necessarily primary or explicitly allocated but passively delegated functions which bus stations deliver. These will also be discussed as part of this section.

As explained by the station designer, various elements designed that restrict the use of bus stations and also the corridor to 'only BRTS' have been depicted in Figure 4.4 to Figure 4.9 (Arya, 2014).

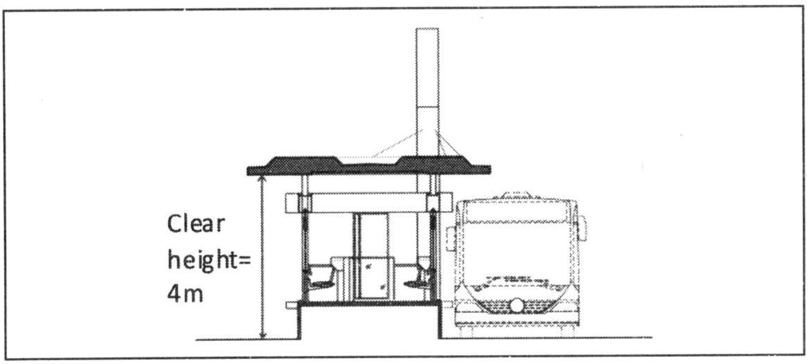

Source: BRTS Design Team, CRDF.

Fig. 4.4: BRT station elements — roof limit vehicles higher than 4m

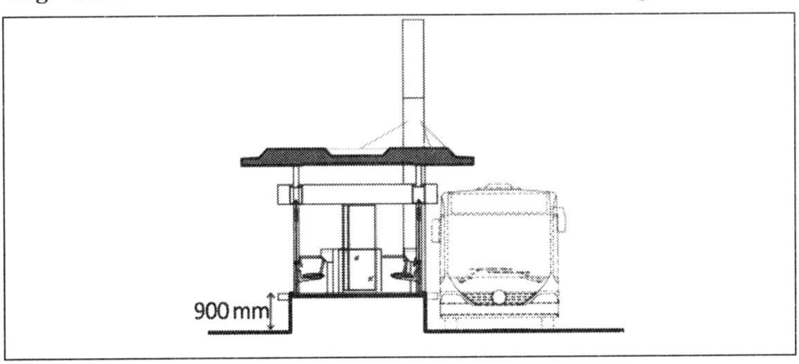

Source: BRTS Design Team, CRDF.

Fig. 4.5: BRT station elements — station floor height limit at 900 mm

As depicted in Figure 4.4, the roof height of the bus station has been designed to give a clearance of 4 metres, which is adequate to clear an AC bus but not a regional bus with luggage laden on it or laden trucks.

Figure 4.5 depicts that the floor height of the station is fixed at 900 mm and the bus floor is also built to the same height. This limits the use of stations with floor height other than 900 mm and right side door on the bus.

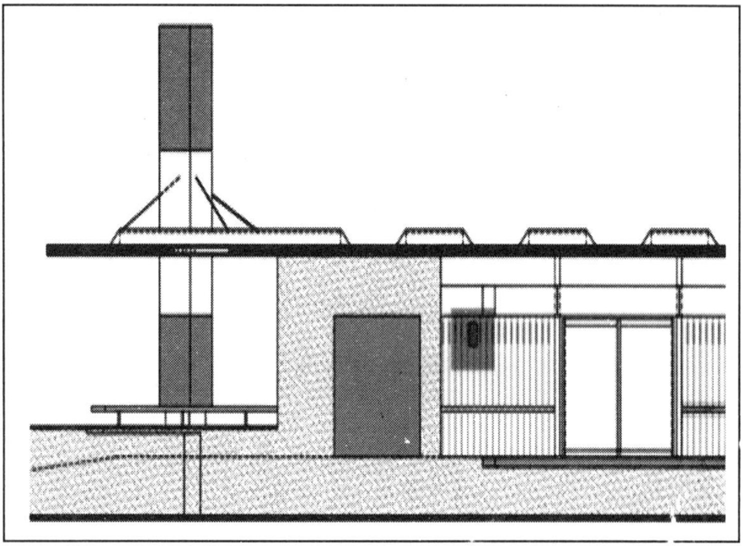

Source: BRTS Design Team, CRDF.

Fig. 4.6: RFID readers at both the shelter and on the bus enaole opening of automated doors

RFID readers are used to control access to stations and buses. RFID is put at both the shelter and on the bus, enabling opening of automated doors. In the case of regular buses, doors will be on the left side. This controls the docking location as well as station and bus doors.

Buses are equipped with GPS systems and it enables the monitoring of the bus system through the control centre. In this process, the exact location of the bus vis-à-vis the station is identified and passenger announcements both on the bus and at the stations are made.

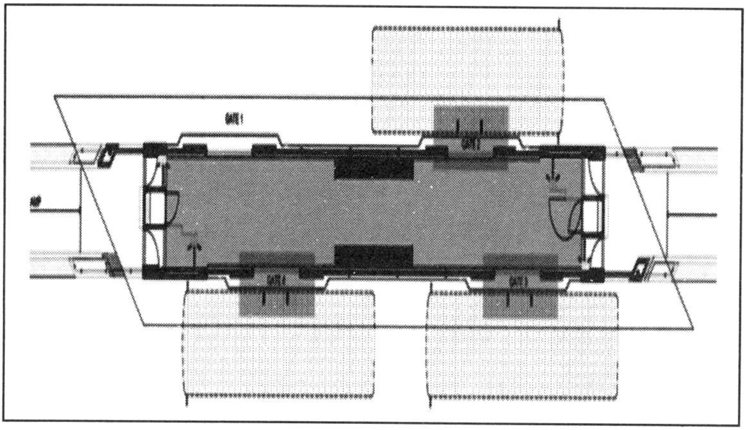

Source: BRTS Design Team, CRDF.

Fig. 4.7: Design excludes regular buses with left side doors; shelter accessed with BRT buses having doors to the right.

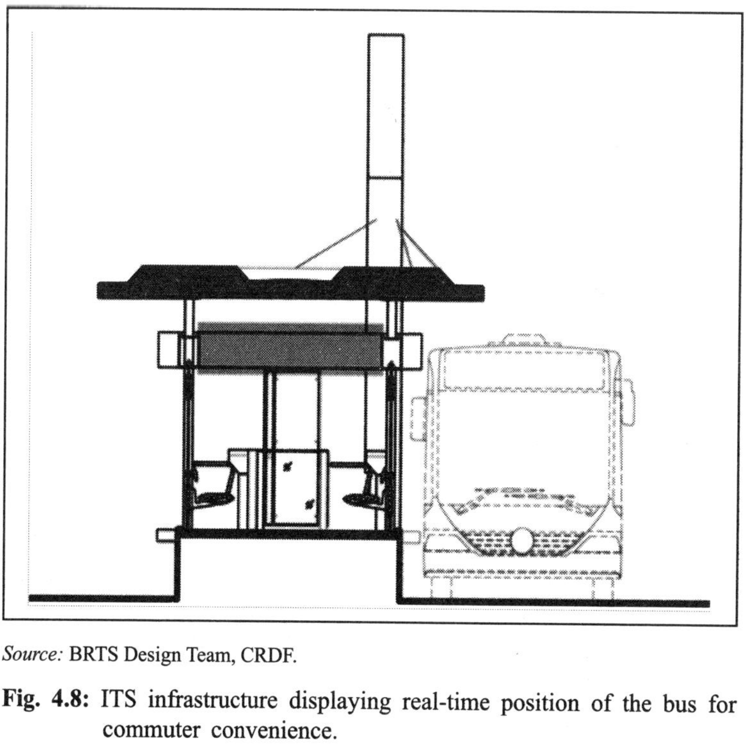

Source: BRTS Design Team, CRDF.

Fig. 4.8: ITS infrastructure displaying real-time position of the bus for commuter convenience.

Ahmedabad BRTS was the first bus system to adopt an off-board automatic ticketing system. In addition to reducing dwell time for buses, it also prevents unauthorised entry, adding to the security of the passengers.

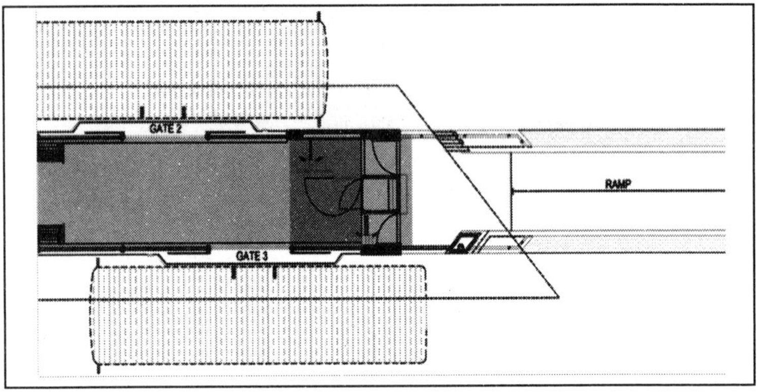

Source: BRTS Design Team, CRDF.

Fig. 4.9: External ticketing and flap gates to check authorised entry.

4.5.1 *Spacing*

Spacing of bus stations is a critical decision. Closely spaced stations are more accessible but impact bus performance in terms of speed and fuel consumption. Stations located far apart would mean faster mobility, but people would have to walk a longer distance. Depending on the mode, a trade-off is made. On regular city bus services, bus stations (they are called stops) are generally 300-400 metres apart (AMTS). In the case of metro systems, the station spacing is about 1-1.2 km. For the Ahmedabad BRT, in order to balance accessibility and performance, considering a five-minute walking distance, the designers fixed the spacing of bus stations at 500-600 metres from each other.

4.5.2 *Location*

Conventional bus stations, two in number, are designed for the kerb side (mostly one opposite the other) and serve the purpose of accommodating passengers travelling in opposite directions. The BRTS Ahmedabad bus stations, on the other hand, were designed as a single built space in the centre of the road ('Island Stations'). The scheme of providing two separate bus stations in the centre of the road for people travelling in opposite directions was discarded in favour of the single median bus stations, which are spacious as they utilise the space for two stations in a single space. The reduction in cost achieved by building just one bus station at a location instead of two was a consideration for the decision. Single bus stations also reduced the cost in terms of maintenance and operations (e.g. the number of staff to be employed).

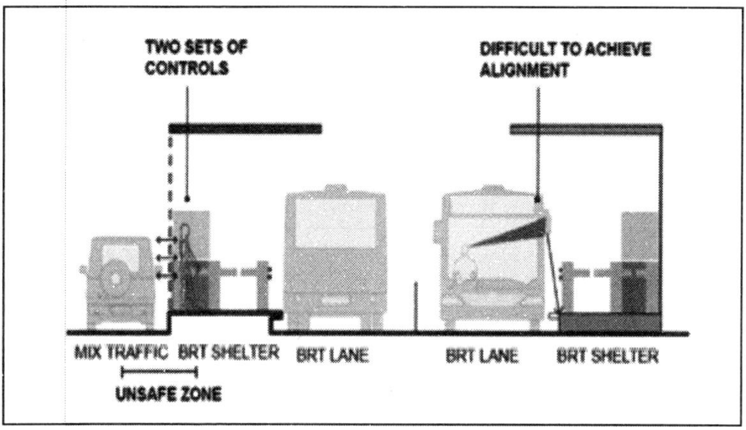

Source: BRTS Design Team, CRDF.

Fig. 4.10: Kerb-side bus station

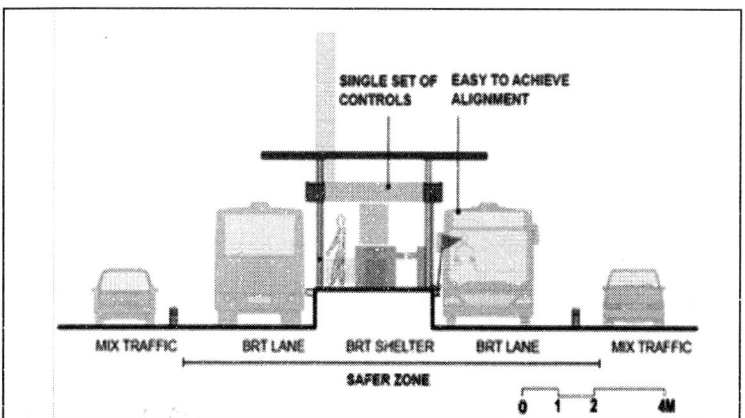

Source: BRTS Design Team, CRDF.

Fig. 4.11: Median bus station

The design of the single median bus station had issues regardless of its advantages. It was for the first time that people in the city were exposed to using a single bus station for both directions. The BRTS bus stations were provided with information display boards and real-different directions but also the route details.

4.5.3 *Impact of Floor Height on Bus Station Infrastructure*

It is important to match the bus station floor height with the bus floor height to achieve at-level boarding and alighting of passengers and barrier-free access. The bus station plinths, therefore, vary, as shown in Table 4.2. The length of ramps provided to access bus stations also vary, considering minimum 1:14 gradient recommended as per IRC standards.

Table 4.2: Floor height of bus station infrastructure

Sl. No.	Bus floor height	Type	Bus station ramp length (1:14)
1	400 mm	Low floor	5.6 m
2	650 mm	Semi-low floor	9.1 m
3	900 mm	High floor	12.6 m
4	1150 mm	High floor	16.1 m

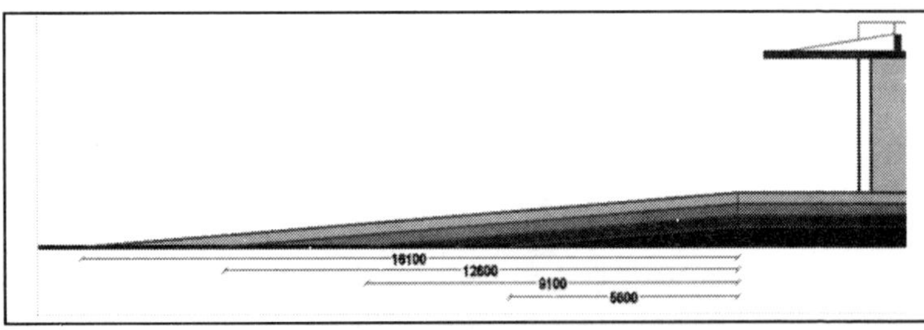

Source: BRTS Design Team, CRDF.

Fig. 4.12: Ramp lengths with reference to floor levels

Figure 4.12 suggests that for bus stations of a lower floor height, the ramp length and height are reduced, hence the infrastructure cost, too, goes down. On the other hand, with lower station-floor height and a smaller ramp, access to the station is closer to the docked bus, which is visually blocked by the station façade and hence the safety of passengers exiting the median station is compromised as they try to cross the bus lane.

Another aspect of safety in level boarding is passenger behaviour. For low-height bus stations (i.e. 400 mm high), it is easy for commuters to step down and climb, hence it is difficult to control station access from the bus lane. For example, in the case of Pune's low BRT stations, commuters climb down on the bus-lane and wait for their respective buses. Station floor height of 650 mm is inconvenient for commuters to climb up or down, whereas 900 mm is downright difficult. (Refer Figure 4.13).

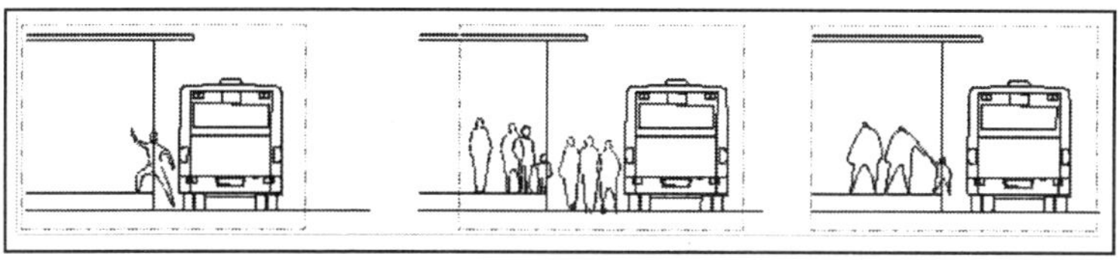

Source: BRTS Design Team, CRDF.

Fig. 4.13: Floor height: 400 mm (left side door docking)

In the case of low-floor buses, the bus station floor height too would be as low as 400 mm. As a result, the chances of people getting on and off the bus stations directly from the sides and into the bus lanes is high, as illustrated in Fig. 4.14. This is extremely unsafe for the passengers waiting at the bus stations, especially children. Also, in the case of low-lying areas with chances of water accumulation and flood prone situations, these buses should be avoided as they disrupt the services. The road conditions such as levelling and speed breakers also need to be conditioned to allow smooth rides for 400 mm floor buses.

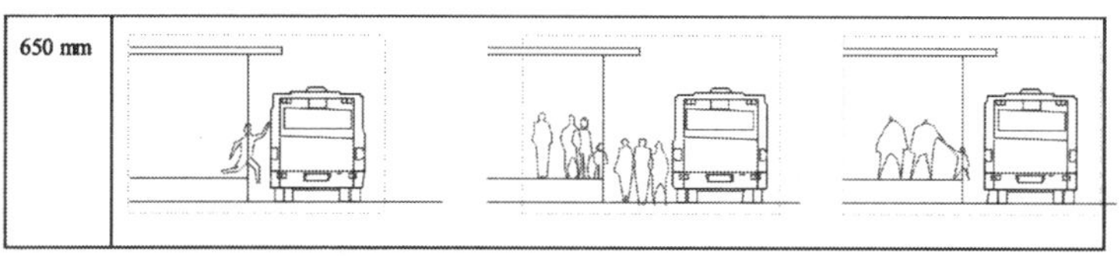

Source: BRTS Design Team, CRDF.

Fig. 4.14: Floor height: 650 mm (left-side door docking)

In the case of medium-floor (i.e. 650 mm) bus stations, it is more difficult to climb from the bus lane onto the bus station; however, people may jump or get down from the bus station on to the bus lane. This is also an unsafe condition (Refer Figure 4.15).

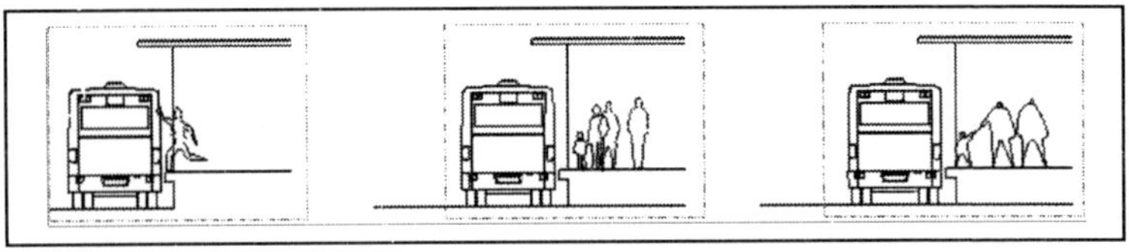

Source: BRTS Design Team, CRDF.

Fig. 4.15: Floor height: 900 mm floor height (Right-side door docking)

In the case of 900 mm high floor bus stations, this condition of passenger infiltration to and from the bus lanes to bus stations and vice versa is prevented. Because of this, the passengers get controlled access through ramps on both sides of the bus station. Access controls can be implemented while maintaining barrier-free access through right-side doors, as was adopted in the Ahmedabad BRTS (Refer Figure 4.16).

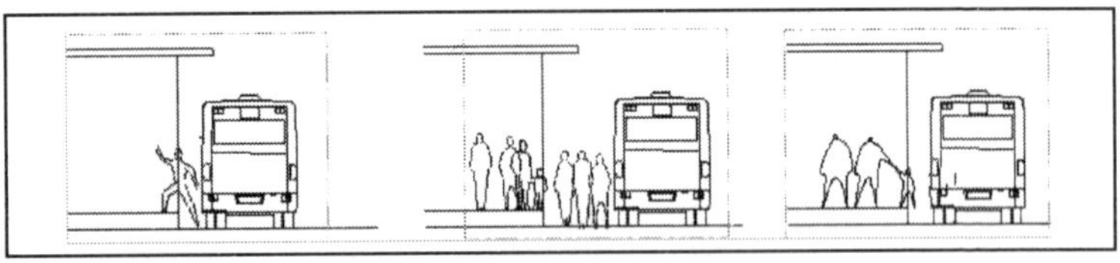

Source: BRTS Design Team, CRDF.

Fig. 4.16: Floor height: 1150 mm (left-side door docking)

In the case of 1150 mm high floor buses, with docking facility on the left-side door, the first step height needs to be at 400 mm level. As a result, the conditions similar to 400 mm-high floor buses emerge in this alternative. As discussed earlier, the chances of people getting on and off the bus stations directly from the sides rather than the using the ramps and spillage in bus lanes is high.

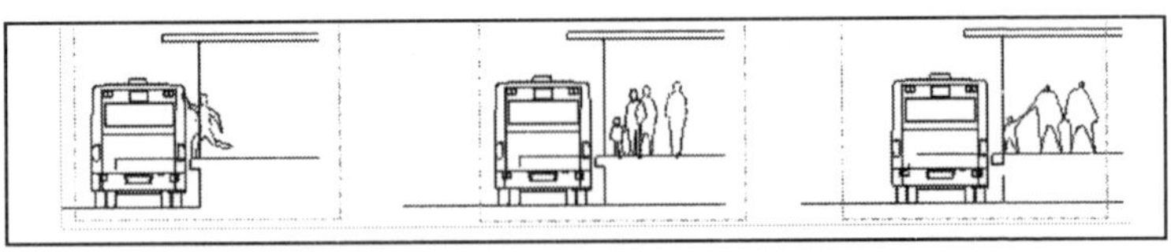

Source: BRTS Design Team, CRDF.

Fig. 4.17: Floor height: 1150 mm (right-side door docking)

In the case of 1150 mm high-floor buses, with docking facility at the right-side door, the bus station floor height may be provided at 1150 mm level. As in the case of 900 mm high bus stations, the at-level boarding and alighting is achieved. Conditions for spillage on to the bus lanes do not exist, hence this would be a safe option. At present, however, there are no systems using 1150 mm high buses with right-side doors, but this option could be explored.

4.5.4 *Access to high plinth bus stations*

Breaking away from the conventional kerb-side bus station design, the primary design requirement for the BRT was to ensure ease of access to the stations in the centre of the road. Stations, mostly located near traffic junctions, were built to have an approach from the junction side, regulated by synchronised traffic signals and zebra crossings.

Fig. 4.18: Access to median bus station through zebra crossings

The continuous railings on the median that provide exclusive access to the BRT lanes only to BRT buses, are punctured at the bus stations to allow passenger entry. These openings need to restrict vehicular entry, and hence are controlled by bollards.

4.5.5 *Wheelchair Access*

The bollard spacing at the entry to the bus stations is such that it allows wheelchair access. In the beginning, it was observed that two-wheelers attempted to cross the streets at these locations. A staggered alignment of the bollards was thus adopted so as to allow the entry of wheel-chair users but restrict two-wheelers from taking advantage of these openings near the bus stations (see Figure 4.19). In a city where road users show little regard for traffic regulations, the bollard design at the BRT bus stations is an example of how artifacts can shape human behaviour through the use of design.

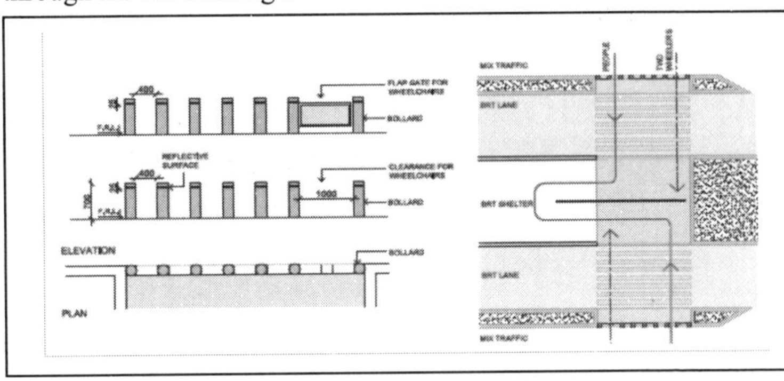

Fig. 4.19: Wheelchair access

4.5.6 *Closed Bus Stations*

The number of passengers travelling without tickets on public transport services in the country is fairly high. Considering what the passengers could afford, a fare structure that matched the existing fare of the city bus service was worked out. An effort was also made to ensure that passengers travelled by paying the fare, and that buying tickets became a habit. The BRT stations were designed as closed bus stations, which allow entry only to passengers with tickets or smart cards. Ticket counters placed at both entry points, and the installation of turnstiles ensured external ticketing. Off-board ticketing for buses was new in the Indian context. BRT staff operating and guiding passengers on the use of turnstiles also ensured the correct use of the ticketing system. The combined efforts of the non-human artifacts and the station guards thus enabled a flawless fare payment system. This convenient and quick payment of fare at the bus stations added to the ease of managing passengers aboard the buses.

4.6 Bus Docking and Boarding/Alighting Controls

The BRT system was designed and implemented to ensure the highest quality of bus-based public transport system that offers passengers a rapid and quality travel experience. The bus is also an artifact, the design of which has been presented in detail in the next chapter.

BRT buses dock on the right side of the buses, and so also have their doors on the right side, unlike the conventional buses that dock on the left side. This design decision was taken following the Bogota model of BRT service. The city government sought to ensure that old AMTS buses could not use the new BRT corridor or its infrastructure. In this manner, the old buses with their doors on the left side were technically handicapped in docking at the bus stations. Likewise, the BRT buses could not leave the corridor and pick up passengers from anywhere other than the BRT bus stations.

This is an example of reconfiguration of agency between various actants (the existing bus service, the new BRT service and the related infrastructure) with the aim of insulating the new and old system from each other. Negotiations on shifting the existing AMTS buses, which plied along BRT corridors prior to the commencement of BRT operations, to other routes in the city were done by the city government. "The design, construction and operation of urban transport systems constitute a process where the actors involved negotiate and actively distribute agency in the components of the new system" (Valderrama & Jorgensen, 2008: 200). This distribution of agency between the existing and proposed public transport in the city was such that the existing city bus service would be allotted new routes which would intersect BRT corridors and act as feeder service to the BRT system.

During brainstorming conducted with the group of various transport experts and at the stage of design and plan finalisation of BRTS implementation, one major concern caught the attention of the stakeholders. The concern related to the open areas meant to align with the bus door at the boarding/alighting area at the bus station, which could be potentially dangerous spots for the commuters.

The challenge was how to avoid mishaps such as passengers at the stations accidently falling off from the open space. The logical solution to avoid such accidents was to have doors in those open spaces that would open only when the bus arrived.

While door installation was identified as the solution to ensure passenger safety, a further challenge was to figure out how the station doors would be operated. It would not be practical for the passengers to open and close the station doors every time they boarded or got off a bus. One option was to hire a person to manage the station doors, but this was not a foolproof solution as there were possibilities of human indiscipline, error and delay. Another option was to give the ticket operator control to operate the doors, but this too was not seen as a viable alternative because it might be too demanding to expect the person to issue tickets as well as manage the door and could lead to a chaotic situation.

What was needed was a machine-managed door operation that would ensure precision in time and docking distance. During the brainstorming sessions, the bus driver was identified as the only person who could decide exactly when to operate the door. It was thus decided that the controls to operate the station as well as the bus doors should be provided to him. The question now was how the driver would know the precise distance and time to dock the bus at the station since he would not have the required view to manage this operation. How would he also ensure that the bus and station boarding levels were aligned and that the distance between the bus and the station was close enough for the passengers to safely board/alight from the bus? The system needed horizontal and vertical distance measurements at a comfortable tolerance level for the buses to dock at the station. The system thus needed not only automated controls with the driver to manage the station/bus doors, but also an efficient and effective docking system management. Clearly, an innovative process was needed in the BRT system which would serve not only passenger safety concerns, but would also set a benchmark for BRT in other cities to follow.

The technology needed to look specifically at the following artifacts while designing a system to offer the passengers a safe and wholesome experience.

- Bus needs to stop within a particular safe zone within the docking area.
- System needs to be able to precisely measure vertical and horizontal distance from the docking area.
- The bus and station doors need to be aligned precisely.

- The bus door and the station door need to be operated synchronously.
- The door operation needs to be wireless as it has to be operated by the driver.

In order to meet the above-stated requirements, the design needed to have the following capabilities:

- Electronic bus identity.
- Sensor for detecting the bus.
- Electronic distance measurement capability.
- Wireless gate operations.
- Driver equipment for door operations.

The Bus Docking and Automated Doors operation at Ahmedabad BRTS was done using of Radio Frequency Identification (RFID) technology. The components used in this technology are:

- Low-frequency (LF) 125KHz RFID reader at the doors.
- LF tag on the bus side window glass near driver.
- RF 2.4 GHz wireless transmitter on the bus driver for Open/ Close operation of the door.
- RF 2.4 GHz 4-door receiver at the station for door control and communication to the door operator.

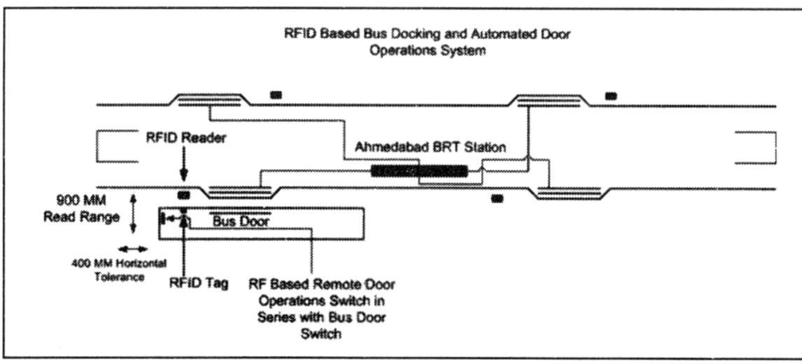

Source: BRTS Design Team, CRDF.

Fig. 4.20: RFID-based bus docking and automated door operations system

The RFID-based solution was selected primarily for the automated door operations for the reason that it offers ease of wireless operation. The RFID TAG allows unique tagging of all buses with electronic numbers, which facilitates the identification of assets owned by Janmarg and offers the security that only Janmarg assets can operate the automated doors. The chosen RFID product allows vertical read range of 90 mm, which is within the tolerance limit of operating the system within the lane; if the same bus is outside the corridor, the door will not operate. The system also allows precision in horizontal tolerance of 400 mm with regard to the station door, which means that the bus can dock on the docking station with a tolerance of 200 mm forward or backward. This horizontal scanning ensures that the bus door and the station door open only if safe opening passage is available.

The RF remote switch, which is installed on the driver's dashboard, is connected with the bus door, thus ensuring that the driver controls both the doors by using a single open/close command.

RFID and RF switches offer a unique combination of a robust solution, keeping in mind the tolerance limits required to operate the doors. RFID tagging also allows asset identification uniquely, and it can thus be used as a fall-back mechanism in case of GPS outages, for maintenance, accessing non-operational buses etc. The TAG will be used in the future to identify and allow access to buses in the depots designated for them. Janmarg could operate boom barriers using this tag based on the authorisation of locations pertaining to those buses.

4.1.6 *Realised benefits of RFID*

- Optimised docking system management by getting more done in less time and with fewer resources.
- Greater visibility and information sharing with the use of advanced technologies and equipment.
- Transportation operators do not have to focus on fare collection but only on the operation of the transportation system.
- It provides information to the transportation authorities regarding delays in service, which can lead to schedule changes and reduction in passenger inconvenience.
- Accuracy in vehicle tracking and scheduling.

4.7 BRTS Operating System

Two kinds of BRT systems are distinguishable — open and closed. The choice of this is a matter of debate and discussion amongst professionals (Gautam, Swamy, Lokre, & Arya, 2014).

- In a 'closed system' of operations, infrastructure and service operations are tied together, and hence greater management control is possible.
- In an 'open system' of operations, as the requirement is only that of a bus lane, infrastructure and operations are delinked.

Service Operations: Benefits and Dis-benefits

- In a closed system, BRTS operations are limited to the network and the (BRTS) buses ply exclusively inside the corridor and benefit from the dedicated infrastructure. As the schedules are carefully planned for optimal use of the infrastructure, operations control is more achievable and schedule predictability is possible. Such systems involve external ticketing, level boarding, and operations monitoring and control. The travel speeds of these systems are, therefore, higher. However, a closed system of operation requires major restructuring of services (routes) and reform in bus operators and operations, which is often a difficult task in the Indian context. In a closed system, given the trunk and feeder arrangements, it is possible to concentrate high frequency service on the trunk corridor.
- In an open system of operations, all buses — BRTS or otherwise — are allowed the benefit of the infrastructure, and buses ply in and out of the corridor depending on the routes. In this kind of system, since the buses ply in and out of the corridor, schedule control is not possible. The advantage, however, is that existing routing and schedules can continue to operate with the new infrastructure. Further, it minimises the requirement for passenger transfers. In an open system, services are likely to be spread thinly over a large part of the network. Therefore, while the open system provides for physical accessibility, service accessibility tends to be low due to low frequency.

The objective of the Ahmedabad BRTS was to provide superior-quality service; the designers, therefore, opted for a closed system, preferring reliability. Considering the fact that the AMTS had been providing and would continue to provide transit service in Ahmedabad, the designers decided to restructure the system by segregating 'Trunk Services' provided as BRTS and 'Complementary and Feeder Services' provided by the AMTS.

4.8 Discussion

In summary, the design process involved delegation of agency to various artifacts envisaged to be part of the new systems through inscriptions.

Based on the analysis of BRTS Ahmedabad, the following are the important observations:

- The artifacts included corridors, RoW segregation, pavement, railings, pedestrian access, landscape, bus station, its location in the median, its floor height, vertical clearance, doors and their control system, police notification, split-flyovers, signage, fares and their collection systems, operating plan giving exclusivity to BRTS etc.
- Designers developed programmes of action to enable certain type of behaviour by users as well as non-users. Designers inscribe certain scripts developed in accordance with those of their programmes of action.
- It is not always true that designers' programme of action is inscribed. Users have their own programmes of action and they also inscribe them. An example of the same has been illustrated with the pedestrian access/bollard use case.
- Two broad types of programmes of action are distinguished: the first 'developing a bus rapid transit system' and the second 'providing a protective envelope for BRT to perform' (i.e. modulating external environment in favour of BRTS operations).
- The artifacts, however, are not necessarily mutually exclusive and do not act alone. Their inscriptions are such that they are part of the BRTS and also designed to modulate external environment.
- Through delegation of agency to non-humans, the attempt is to make the system durable. Once accepted, the state of the artifact is termed as black-boxed. In this case, it is found that several artifacts were black-boxed; the median stations, 900 mm floor height buses, station and bus door controls etc., may be termed as black-boxed.
- While 900 mm floor-height buses became a norm for urban buses in India, they did not remain exclusive to the BRTS.

- Excluding the existing ones is an important aim for the new ones to be durable. The system designers in Bogota and in Copenhagen also made the new systems different and independent of the existing ones: the high platform in Bogotá and the automation in Copenhagen make the new systems completely incompatible with the old ones (Valderrama & Jorgensen, 2008). Similarly, the designers in Ahmedabad also designed high platform, right-side door, door control systems inside the bus etc., however, some of these, with time, developed some leakages.
- These include right-side door of the bus (now AMTS also has similar doors), railing, pedestrian access, artifacts designed to limit entry of other vehicles into the corridor — police notification, operating plan etc. In order to plug leaky artifacts, newer artifacts are designed and/or script is assigned to humans (BRTS police). However, humans are the least durable. Additionally, artifacts such as swing gates and video based monitoring and fines are now under consideration.
- This essentially implies that the system once stabilised will not necessarily remain at that state during the project life cycle. Some actors revolt, some artifacts turn leaky and hence focal actors need to be watchful and build their responses on a continual basis.
- It is evident from this discussion that the designers tend to have many programmes of action for a single intent/objective. Similarly, a single programme may be aimed at multiple intents/objectives. For instance, in Ahmedabad, when the BRT was being designed, the effort was to design special bus lanes. Instead of adopting a 'do-minimum' approach to developing bus lanes, the designers adopted a 'complete street' approach. This resulted in multiple positive outcomes for the city. In addition to the BRT system, it improved mobility for personalised vehicle users, resulting in an effective traffic management system, and contributed to improvements in the area along BRT corridors. Increased land value as a result of changing land uses, and the value capture potential have been auxiliary but intended benefits of the programme. While the intent was to develop the BRT, several other auxiliary benefits emerged as part of the design process.

- A single programme of action may have multiple scripts, and multiple programmes of action may be achieved through a single script. Similarly, multiple artifacts may be used to inscribe a single script. The repetitive layers would enhance the strength of the protection envelope (in the case of BRT), making inscriptions stronger through layers of artifacts with the same script. Scripts may be embedded into the artifact or the artifact may accompany the script. For example, bus station is embedded with the script to enable level boarding, while a police notification display is an artifact which accompanies the script.

NOTE

1. Detail Project Report was prepared in 2005, and formally submitted to Government of India in 2007.

5
Deciding Janmarg Vehicle
Distribution of Agency

5.1 Introduction

As buses are in direct interaction with the end users and define the identity of the system, they form a critical element of the Bus Rapid Transit System. The design of the bus would have to take into consideration multiple requirements. The characteristics of the BRT vehicle can be observed from the perspective of commuters, operator, regulator and the community as a whole. For a 'user' the importance of the vehicle is for the commute experience, while for a 'system operator' the vehicle design is critical as it affects the operational efficiency and costs. System developers would look at measurable social benefits in terms of environment, safety and ridership.[1]

At the time when Ahmedabad was planning its BRTS (2005-06), the automobile industry was not as advanced in the country as it is today. There were no bus manufacturers who built a bus in its complete form. The common practice was that small-scale industries (Coach Builders) procured truck chassis from automobile manufacturers to fabricate buses on them. The buses thus built were high floor (1100+ mm floor height). As the coach builders were building buses as per the requirements of individuals and agencies, there was no standardisation of bus components. Hence each bus was different in its design in some way or the other. Some private bus operators had experimented with imported buses to ply on long distance inter-city routes. For city transport service, however, importing buses was an expensive option owing to high price differentials between the Indian market and European or Latin American markets.[2]

Initially, the project designers had thought that once the type and size of the bus was decided, selecting the bus would be a simple process of identifying the best bus manufactured in the country, and procuring it through a tender process. But instead of just selecting a 'bus,' in reality it became a multi-actor, multi-stage and recursive design process with extended time lines. This chapter, adopting the ANT lens, especially the 'distribution of agency,' attempts to explain how Ahmedabad city designed its BRT bus.

This chapter has been divided into four sections. A review of state-of-the-art technology was done through market scanning, literature review, and consultations with technical experts and manufacturers. This, along with other relevant issues, has been presented in Section 5.2. The section also presents the conclusions of a technical workshop that was held to discuss bus design. Section 5.3 describes how bus specifications were finalised and the buses were procured. During this process, at an early stage of project development, it was decided to use the private sector for bus operations. The final section 5.4, deals with this aspect along with discussing the process and drawing some conclusions.

5.2 Vehicle Technology

The project design team had developed a working paper which reviewed both the requirements of BRT and the state-of-the-art vehicle technology. Along with this, an inventory of various bus models manufactured in India was also appended. The working paper (CEPT & GIDB) was used as a basis for discussion on bus technology. A workshop was organised by CEPT on 28 October, 2005 to assess various BRT vehicle options available in India. The workshop participants included key political and executive decision-makers from the city and the state, and the heads of Indian vehicle manufacturing companies. Technical experts from the field were also invited (See Appendix 4 for summary proceedings of the workshop). From the discussions, four important aspects of vehicle design emerged that influenced the choice of vehicle: capacity of the bus, floor height of the bus, engine power and location of engine, and fuel choice. These factors are further discussed in this section.

5.2.1 *Capacity and External Dimensions*

Several factors influence vehicle design and selection. These include service demand, frequency of service, average vehicle speed and its load factor, route length, average passenger load, passenger preference in terms of comfort level and their paying capability etc.

Table 5.1: Bus size, headway and passenger capacity

Bus Type	Length (metres)	Width (metres)	Typical Capacity* (Seating + Standing)	Peak hour peak direction passengers carried for headways (minutes)[3]				
				1	2	3	5	10
Mini	≤ 7	2.2	16-24	1440	720	480	288	144
Midi	9 + 0.4	2.2	27-40	2400	1200	800	480	240
Standard	12 + 0.1	2.6	60-70	4200	2100	1400	840	420
Articulated	18	2.6	110-140	8400	4200	2800	1680	840
Bi articulated	24	2.6	210-220	13200	6600	4400	2640	1320

Source: Computed by Author.

The system capacity also depends on bus capacity. The market provided scope for adopting mini, midi, regular, articulated and bi-articulated size buses, that is, buses appropriate for passenger capacity ranging from 18 to 170 persons. The option of articulated buses, however, did not exist within the country.[4] In addition to availability of a vehicle, its capital and operating costs, availability and amount of funding, and the expected demand appear to play key roles in choosing the vehicle type. At the time of project development, no programmes of the Government of India or of the Government of Gujarat provided support for procurement of buses. Hence, the local body had to find its own funding source for procuring BRT buses.

Given the level of demand, trade-off is made between the size (capacity) of the bus and the headway/frequency. The design team had projected a total of 4 lakh boardings as the demand in the near future (2021) and estimated a requirement of 200 buses to operate on the phase-1 and phase-2 networks of about 85 km.[5] The estimate of Peak Hour Peak Direction Traffic (PHPDT) was that it would begin in the range of 5000 to 8000. With one lane in each direction, it was expected that a standard 12-metre bus would be sufficient to serve the estimated demand.

5.2.2 *Bus Floor Height*

Floor height influences boarding and alighting speed, which controls the dwell time of the bus at the bus station, simplicity and ease of access, and safety of the passengers. At the time when Ahmedabad was making a decision about the bus, there were two options available in floor height — low floor (380 mm) and high floor (1100-1150 mm). Since then, there have been two additions to the floor levels of buses. The first is the standard floor (900 mm, flat floor) height bus which was designed for Ahmedabad's BRTS, and the second is a semi-low floor (650 mm) height bus.

Each of the options may be described as no-step entry (low floor), one-step (semi-low floor), two-step (standard floor) and three-step (high floor) buses. The standard height of a step is about 250 mm (refer Appendix 5).

5.2.2.1 *High-floor buses*

These were the buses built on truck chassis with a floor height ranging from 1000 mm to 1150 mm above the pavement, i.e. three steps of 200 to 250 mm each above the entry level of 400 mm. There are several advantages of this type of bus. The engine can be accommodated under the floor along with the fuel tank, other electrical equipment as well as the CNG cylinders, if CNG is the chosen fuel. The floor is entirely flat which results in an increase in the number of seats and in the overall capacity, and also more efficient movement within the bus. These buses are also inexpensive to build and maintain.

High-floor buses, however, are inconvenient to board and add significantly to the boarding and alighting time. Although high-floor buses can be equipped with a bridge, rapidly deployable ramp, door flap or high platform to reduce conjunction and dwell time, simultaneous operation of the same bus on exclusive corridors (with high platforms) and on other corridors (without platform) would be problematic.

5.2.2.2 *Low-floor buses*

In 2001, the Maharashtra High Court, while hearing a public interest litigation (PIL) filed by students of a Pune Law College, the Indian Law Society, seeking better facilities for the disabled, especially in the public transport sector, had directed all transport undertakings in the state to seek its permission before purchase of new buses. The Court had imposed this condition to ensure that the transport sector complied with the provisions of the Persons with Disabilities Act (*Times of India*, 2004). This triggered the development of low-floor buses in India, with BEST placing a purchase order with Tata Motors Limited on a competitive bidding.

These buses have a floor height of 380–400 mm from the ground, a 70 mm kneeling facility on the left side to bring down the floor height to 310 mm at the entrance/exit, and a manually operated, light-weight and slip-resistant ramp for wheelchairs. They also have an extra-wide middle door, 1000 mm compared to the 850 mm wide doors of regular buses, and can accommodate two wheelchairs at a time. The first lot of buses were deployed in August 2005 by BEST. These were also the first buses fully manufactured in the country.

Low-floor buses are, in effect, low-entry buses and inside the bus at least 50 per cent, and up to 70 per cent, of the total saloon area is low floor (excluding front wheel boxes and the driver's cab) and is not ramped in the longitudinal plane. As per Urban Bus Specification, one hundred per cent low floor buses are technically feasible but their costs would be prohibitive, and in India, they are not even used at airports.

The limitations of low-floor buses far outnumber the advantages. A major advantage of these buses is that they provide for easy and speedy boarding and alighting. But the flow inside the bus would not be smooth because passengers would have to negotiate three levels. There is no space under the floor to accommodate the engine, fuel tanks and electrical equipment, which are accommodated behind the bus, taking up the space of four to six seats. CNG cannot be accommodated under the floor, and the gas cylinders have to be mounted on the top of the vehicle, requiring a sturdier body design. The placement of the cylinders on the top also makes refuelling difficult, and adds to the capital, maintenance and operating costs.

Low-floor buses require driveways that are smooth and without interruptions, which is difficult to achieve in India. In terms of operations and maintenance costs, low floor buses are more expensive than standard buses. The capital cost of low-floor buses too is higher, which is often attributed to the inclusion of product development costs.

5.2.2.3 *Semi-low floor buses*

As stated earlier, this option was not available in India when Ahmedabad BRTS was being designed. By the time the tendering for bus procurement was taken up, however, the mode with 700 mm $\pm$ 50 mm had been designed.

Two main considerations influenced the development of these buses. The first was the increasing emphasis by the public and the court on making buses more accessible. The second was the limitation arising out of the difficulty in urban India of keeping driveways smooth and without interruption for the low-floor buses. As a result, manufacturers explored a mid-way solution by designing the floor height at 650 mm.

The advantages of the semi-low-floor buses are that they are relatively easy to board as passengers have to climb only one step; the fuel tank and electrical equipment fit under the floor, so service problems are reduced and the loss of internal space is prevented.

The disadvantages are similar to those of the low-floor buses. As the semi-low floor buses have their engine at the back of the bus, one has to climb two steps inside the bus to access the rear portion of the saloon. Movement within the buses too is not smooth because of these steps. Increased boarding and alighting times affect dwell times adversely. The engine at the rear also means a reduction of space in terms of two to three seats. The limitation in terms of placing CNG under the body remains and hence, it has to be mounted on top of the vehicle, which makes the vehicle expensive.

5.2.2.4 *Standard-floor buses*

Buses with a standard floor height of 900 mm were also not available when the BRTS was being designed, but the option emerged out of the design process. There had been efforts to design buses with floor height between 400 mm and 1100 mm. Manufacturers attempted 700 mm $\pm$ 50 mm buses as presented above. A variant with 900 mm floor height bus was also being proposed. The 650 mm bus variant was an interesting option but it still contained disadvantages similar to those of a low-floor bus, including the high cost (discussed in detail later). These buses have the engine in the front.

5.2.3 *Vehicle Engine Configuration and Fuel Choice*

Low air and noise emission vehicles are extremely desirable for BRTS, especially in situations where buses frequently converge, such as near or in central business districts (Zimmerman & Levinson, 2007). Three basic types of propulsion systems are generally used for BRT application: internal combustion engines (ICEs); dual mode; diesel-electric and hybrid (IC and electric).

The most commonly used propulsion system for buses is the internal combustion engine (fuelled by diesel, ultra-low sulphur diesel (ULSD) or natural gas). Electric trolley buses (ETBs), though a well-established technology producing zero-emission at the point of use, were not considered. As stated earlier, project planners did not consider importing vehicles as a viable option. This applied to dual fuel vehicles as well.

As a part of the workshop in October 2005, an interesting, locally-manufactured option in the form of a low-floor, hybrid electric bus emerged. An Ahmedabad-based company, Electrotherm (India) Ltd., was in the process of developing such a bus. The presentation looked promising but the timelines appeared to spillover much beyond the project timeline. Further, the project planners were of the view that coupling too many innovations together would multiply the risks of the project, and hence they decided to focus on the primary innovation, i.e. making of the BRTS. Thus, the choice was limited to internal combustion engine fuelled by diesel or natural gas.

5.2.3.1 *Fuel choice*

In India, a major debate on fuel choice for transit emerged as an outcome of a Public Interest Litigation filed by the environmental activist lawyer M.C. Mehta in the Supreme Court in 1996 (Mehta, 2002). At that time, Delhi was rated as the third most polluted city in the world, and actions to mitigate air pollution were to be taken up urgently.

At that time, diesel was a very dirty fuel, with its sulphur content at 1000 ppm (BS-I).[6] The share of diesel-powered vehicles was already high and increasing. As a result, the levels of particulate matter (PM) in the air were found to be high. Further, the levels of NO_x were also found to be rising. Roychowdhury, quoting a World Bank study, pointed out that, in 2004, 'depending on the season, the contribution of diesel fuel to the total PM 2.5 ambient concentration can be as high as 61 per cent in Kolkata, 23 per cent in Delhi and 25 per cent in Mumbai' (Roychowdhury, 2010: 5), and cautioned that 'Indian cities cannot continue to add the high emitters of PM and NO_x, like conventional diesel vehicles.' A comparative picture of emission levels of diesel and CNG as per the fuel standards of BS-II are presented in Table 5.2.

Table 5.2: Comparative emissions of diesel and CNG buses in India

Type of bus	CO g/km	HC g/km	N_{ox} g/km	PM g/km	CO_2 g/km	km/litre
Euro II diesel bus on 500 ppm sulphur fuel + DOC	1.45	0.29	6.24	0.35	798.7	3.33
Euro II diesel bus on 350 ppm sulphur fuel + DOC	0.65	0.15	5.85	0.11	766.1	3.44
Euro II diesel bus on 50 ppm sulphur fuel + CRT	1.42	0.04	13.58	0.009	781.38	3.36
Euro II CNG bus + three way catalytic converter	3.18	1.455	5.35	0.0065	729.74	NA

Source: The Energy and Resource Institute (2004 as cited in Roychowdhury, 2010: 6).

Based on the recommendations of the Environment Pollution (Emission and Control) Authority, set up by the Supreme Court, orders were issued in 1998 for public transport buses and auto-rickshaws plying in Delhi to switch over to the single-fuel mode of CNG by 1 April, 2001.

Subsequently, the Supreme Court expanded the scope to include 14 other cities for monitoring the implementation of strategies for mitigating air pollution, and a committee under Mr. Bhurelal was set up to monitor the progress. Ahmedabad was one of the cities in this list, and CNG conversion was mandated.

5.2.3.2 *Engine power*

Public Transport (PT) services are designed to serve a series of service stops usually located 400 m to 600 m apart in city services. As public transport vehicles require frequent halts, including those at junctions, the pattern of bus movement is 'stop-and-go', i.e. its speed profile is like a wave with multiple halts. In order to minimise journey time by maximising system speed on urban route network, characterised by frequent starts and stops, buses need to be equipped with adequately powered engines to provide the requisite acceleration and gradeability at the rated gross vehicle weight.

Optimal engine power requirement is mainly influenced by Gross Vehicle Weight (GVW), the desired levels of vehicle speed, acceleration and capability to negotiate gradability. It is required that the rated engine power be available at lower rates of crankshaft rotations, i.e. revolutions per minute (rpm), for improved performance in frequent 'stop-and-go' type urban operations. In such operations, the bus engine is further required to have higher torque at lower engine rpm, and the peak torque spread over a wider range of rpm for optimal response.

On the other hand, fuel efficiency may be adversely affected with higher engine horsepower, giving rise to increased operational fuel cost, although the overall efficiency of the system increases with improved speed. Therefore, optimum engine capacity has to be understood in the context of all the requirements. For a standard bus of nearly 16 ton GVW, operating in an obstruction-free environment such as the BRTS, a high-power engine above 200 hp to obtain vehicle acceleration of the order of 0.8-1.0 m/s/s, and gradability levels of 21 per cent at GVW would be required, and are thus proposed for the BRTS. The power requirement would further increase (>230 hp) if the said engine supports a bus air conditioning system.

The impact of acceleration on overall journey speed in a comparatively barrier-free environment of BRTS, i.e. with one stop and one junction per kilometre, is illustrated in Figure 5.1, depicting reduced cruising distances with decreasing acceleration levels, maintaining deceleration at twice the maximum acceleration level in each case. Longer cruising distance facilitates reduction in journey time.

Cruising Distance Assessment (Lakra, Crusing Distance, 2014)

Buses tend to achieve improved speeds and reduced travel time when enabled to operate at cruising speeds over a majority of the distance travelled. In 'start-and-stop' type of urban transit operations, this may be achieved by equipping buses with adequately powered engines delivering maximum torque at lower and wider range of engine rpm, and capable of achieving higher bus acceleration. Buses equipped with such engines reach cruising speeds faster and operate at that speed for longer periods/distances to obtain improved overall speeds, as illustrated in Figure 5.1.

It can be seen from Figure 5.1 that with decreasing levels of bus accelerations, cruising distance is shortened and vice versa. Figure 5.1(a) depicts that with an acceleration of 0.4 m/s/s, a bus runs at cruising speed for only about 80 metres (16 per cent of the distance between stops) as most of the remaining distance between stops is utilised in accelerating to the cruising speed and then decelerating to stop. With an acceleration of 1 m/s/s, on the other hand, a bus runs at cruising speed for nearly 300 metres (60 per cent of the distance between stops), and it achieves cruising speed in a much shorter distance.

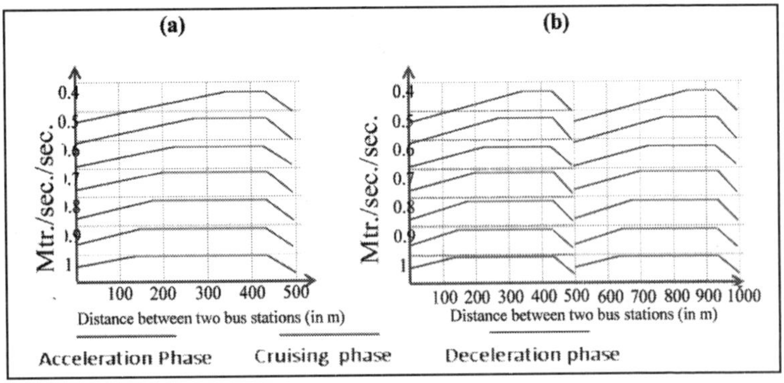

Fig. 5.1: Cruising Distance Assessment

In the above cases, uniform deceleration is considered irrespective of bus acceleration levels. Should deceleration levels be taken as twice those of bus acceleration levels, bus cruising distances would shrink further (except in the case of 1 m/s/s acceleration level where deceleration is already taken as twice that of acceleration). Figure 5.1(b) indicates how, for lower bus acceleration levels, most of a kilometre-long space between stops is utilised for accelerating to cruising speed and then decelerating to stops, with very little space left for bus cruising. Both cases reflect that average bus speeds are low for buses powered to achieve low acceleration levels. Such speeds would be significantly lower when the number of 'stops-and-starts' increases on account of intersections and other interferences or frictions en route.

With increasing acceleration capabilities of buses, the distance and time to achieve cruising speeds decreases, enabling buses to travel at a cruising speed for a longer distance, thereby increasing the overall travel speed. In the above illustrations, as bus acceleration capability increases from 0.4m/s/s to 1m/s/s, the overall bus travel speed increases by nearly 30 per cent-from 32.7 to 42.4 km per hour.

From the above discussion, one can conclude that BRT buses require higher-powered engines when compared to mixed mode operations. Buses equipped with engines optimally powered for achieving high acceleration and torque, efficiently designed, and suitably matched with other sub-systems of a bus, provide superb driveability and optimal fuel economy. Buses thus achieve higher overall speeds, lower turnaround time, improved bus productivity and reduced travel time. Such engines normally offer high torque across a wide range of revolutions per unit time. For instance, a bus equipped with 300 hp engine, delivering a maximum torque of 1400 Nm, provides instant response to the accelerator, quick acceleration and excellent pulling power in high gear. Simply stated, it offers higher levels of commuter comfort and more efficient driving. It delivers best overall performance when matched by a choice of automatic transmissions and rear axles. Such engines tend to be environmentally optimised when built to latest emission norms, say Bharat Stage IV, or as applicable. It is, therefore, necessary to specify higher acceleration levels while designing or acquiring buses for BRT operations.

5.2.4 *Engine location*

Engines may be located in the front or in the rear. Floor height and engine location are interdependent decisions. High (1050-1150 mm) floor and standard floor (900 mm) buses can accommodate engines in the front. These types of buses have been in operation for a long time and hence their maintenance requirements are understood to be simple and easy. In buses with low and semi-low floor, engines have to be located in the rear. Gangway width also gets limited in low and semi-low floor height buses if one desires to take a door on the left side in the front. Rear-engine buses require skilled manpower to maintain them, and as the availability of such facilities with skilled manpower (at the time bus decisions were made) was limited, they were considered risky. Engines may also be located in the middle of a bus, but this is rare in

Indian bus design. The benefits and disadvantages of engine location for commuters, drivers and operators are summarised in Table 5.3.

Table 5.3: Floor height, engine location and impacts on passengers, drivers and operators[7]

Aspect	Low Floor Bus (400 mm)	Semi-Low Floor Bus (650 mm)	Standard Floor Bus (900 mm)	High Floor Bus (1000–1150 mm)
Engine Location	Rear	Rear	Front	Front
Ease of boarding and alighting	High	Moderate	High	High
Ease of movement inside the bus	Low	Low	High	High
Space availability (seats lost when compared to high floor bus)	4-6 seats	2-4 seats	0 seats	0 seats
Driver Comfort (Heat, Vibration)	High	High	Moderate	Moderate
Cost	High	High	Low	Low

Source: Developed by Author.

5.2.4.1 *Internal layout and passenger capacity*

The low and semi-low floor buses in India are typically available with rear engines, because of which the rear portion (30-40 per cent area) of the bus floor is raised up to 1150 mm. Steps inside the bus with 250 mm risers and 230 mm treads provide access to this raised portion where 12 to 15 seats are located. The standing capacity of the bus is, therefore, reduced to between 20 to 25 as the inside gets split at two levels as against the usual standing capacity of 40-50 passengers in a flat-floor bus.

In the case of 900 mm and 1150 mm high floor buses, the option of front engine makes access and movement inside the bus extremely easy as the entire bus floor, except the engine portion in front, is at one level. In the 900 mm high-floor Janmarg buses, the entire bus floor is flat, and with around 36 seats, the standing capacity can go as high as

Sl. No.	Type/Bus floor heights	% of floor area as flat floor	Floor separations in bus layouts	
1	400 mm Low floor	50-60%	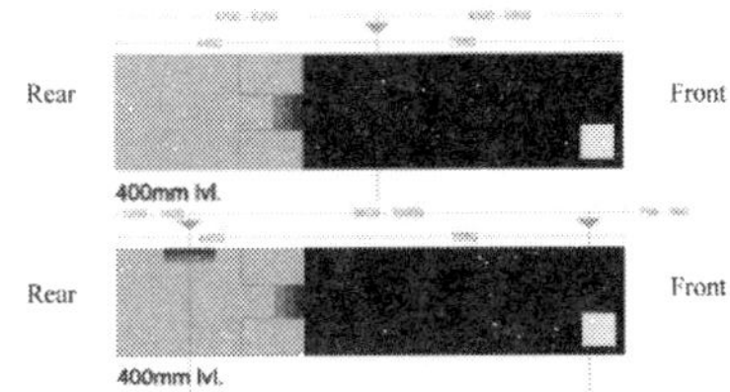	
2	650 mm Semi-low floor	50-60%	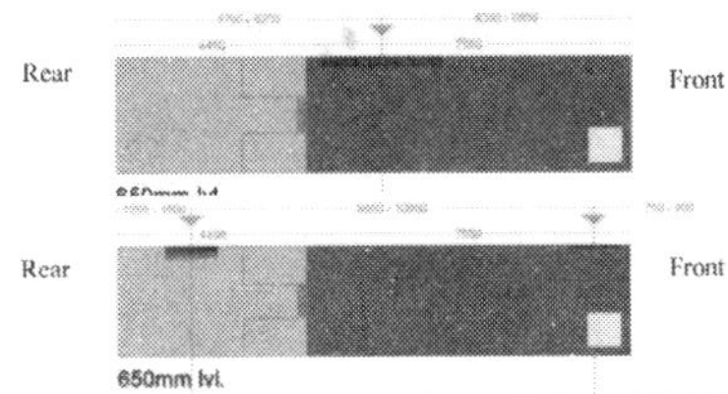	

Source: BRTS Design Team, CRDF.

Fig. 5.2: Specifications for flat-floor buses

Sl. No.	Bus Type floor heights	% of floor area as flat floor	Floor separations in bus layouts	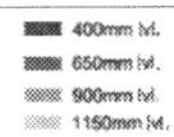
3	900 mm High floor	98% (front engine) - including steps at the entry doors 80–90% (rear engine)	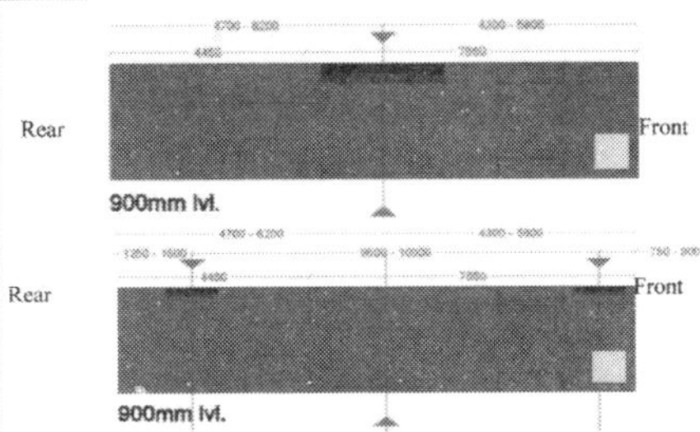	
4	1150 mm High floor	98% (including steps at the entry doors)	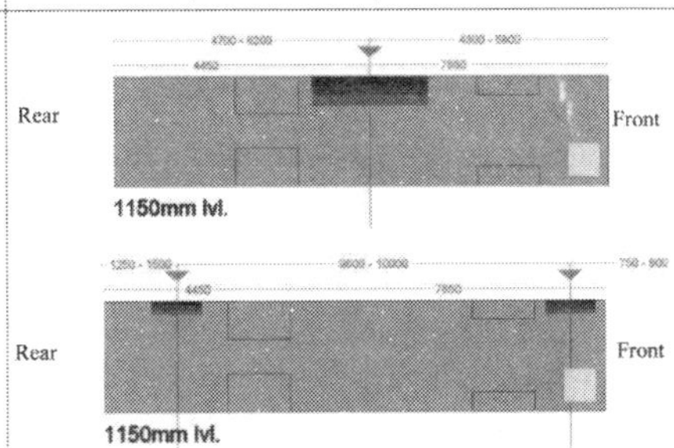	

Source: BRTS Design Team, CRDF.

Fig. 5.3: Bus specifications for floor variation

50 to 60 passengers. There are steps at the entry level of these buses. While entry doors in buses in India are generally on the left side of the bus, in the Janmarg model the buses are accessed from doors on the right side through 900 mm-high-floor bus stations, which offer the highest level of barrier-free accessibility. The left side doors are used only in case of emergencies. In case these buses are used for access from road level or from the left side doors, there are two steps at the bus entry. This, however, creates a friction in passenger movement as they enter the bus and the flow time is increased due to the steps. The entry and exit points have to be separated to reduce the dwell times in such cases, as is followed in several city bus services. High-floor buses are also recommended at locations with low terrain and proneress to flooding or water logging.

5.2.4.2 *Doors: Numbers, positions and type*

With stops every 500 metres, it is important that the bus dwell time at bus stops is kept to the minimum, so that overall vehicle utilisation is increased and system capacity is enhanced. Bus doors, in terms of number, width and placement, and the floor height of the bus determine the boarding and alighting time, i.e. dwell time at the bus stop.

The length of the bus would influence the number and width of the doors. The effort in Ahmedabad for a 12 metre-long bus was to keep two service doors (entrance and exit) in a 1200 mm wide aperture (without flaps). Ease of operations and safety considerations are critical. The entrance and exit doors are, therefore, electro-pneumatically operated with the door lock sensors controlled by the driver, and having internal and external emergency open controls. In the event of an emergency, it is possible to open the doors manually from inside the bus by using a push button control or passing through a light barrier and from outside by an illuminated push button clearly indicating the status. The unlocking devices are clearly marked as an emergency device and require two distinct actions to actuate. Doors, door hinges and locks were chosen to comply with safety requirements as per Indian and international standards. The closing and opening time of the doors is in the range of four seconds. A pilot lamp on the driver's dashboard warns when the door is still 'open' or not fully closed.

There are four basic types of doors available. They are swing door, bi-fold door, pivot door and sliding door. Of these, the first three are recommended as the fourth one is complex and generally riddled with maintenance problems.maintenance problems. Bi-fold doors are used, where a wide opening is required. This type is applied in most BRT buses. Swing doors are simple and easy to deploy, and safe to operate, but they prevent a bus from being stopped close to the edge of a station platform. On the other hand, pivot doors are difficult to use for wide openings because they intrude inside the vehicle.

5.2.4.3 *Floor height and CNG cylinders*

CNG cylinders are generally placed under the floor, which makes refuelling very easy. The space inside the bus gets affected only slightly. In case of leakage of gas, safety problems may arise, but the placement of fuel pipes below the bus helps.

In the case of low-floor and semi-low-floor buses, CNG cylinders have to be placed on top of the bus. Though this is a safe option, the body structure of the bus becomes very heavy due to the cylinder's load. Hence, the cost of the structure increases. Further, refuelling at that height is difficult, and as the fuel pipes are on the outer surface of the bus, they could create safety problems.

5.2.5 ***Workshop Conclusions***

After reviewing presentations on the technical requirements of the buses for Janmarg and the offers from the vehicle manufacturers, the workshop deliberated on several issues. Three main suggestions emerged to guide the further process.

- In terms of floor height, the group recommended low-floor buses as Ahmedabad's BRT vehicle.
- Given the deteriorating air quality in the city and the parallel developments in terms of Supreme Court involvement in monitoring air quality, CNG should be chosen as the fuel.
- The group suggested that specifications should be detailed to an extent that the affordability of such buses could be verified beforehand.

5.3 Design and Procurement of Buses

As noted in Chapter 3, AMC's experience of owning and operating buses under the Ahmedabad Municipal Transport Service had not been encouraging. Year after year, the AMTS has been incurring huge losses. An alternate operational strategy was to be thought of through the involvement of the private sector. Hence, the design process of buses was clubbed with the process of procurement of buses and their operator.

5.3.1 *The Process: Design, Procurement of Buses and Bus Operator*

AMTS had adopted the Public Private Partnership (PPP) model to operate bus services in the city in 2005. As per the agreement, bus procurement, maintenance and operations were carried out by the private operators. AMTS controlled the operations, and operators were paid not by the number of passengers, but by the bus kilometres. A capital subsidy was also given to the bus operator for purchase of buses in the initial phase. Later, the capital subsidy was done away with in subsequent applications. This, in management parlance, is known as the 'Gross Cost Contract (GCC)' model (Ministry of Urban Developement, 2008).

This model received favourable response from decision-makers because it removed the problem of competition on the street. On-street competition is known to increase the safety risk on the road as many operators compete for their share of the market (e.g., Delhi's Red Line and Blue Line buses in the 1990s). The operators were paid by the bus kilometres operated as part of the operations plan provided by AMTS. Nearly 400 buses operated under this model in Ahmedabad at the time when decisions regarding the BRTS bus were being discussed. These were high-floor CNG buses (as mandated by the Supreme Court Committee). Given this experience, the AMC decided to invite private parties to operate the buses.

5.3.2 *Selection of the Bus and the Bus Operator: First Effort*

To ensure fair competition in the bidding process, it was decided to issue an Expression of Interest (EoI), to be followed by a request for proposals, to which seven potential bidders responded. Encouraged by the response, the AMC went ahead with the process of tendering, with the low-floor CNG bus as the chosen technology (Detailed specifications are attached in Appendix 2).

5.3.2.1 *Request for proposals*

A request for proposals (RFP) was published on March 2, 2008. Bids were invited for the 'Charge per Kilometre' operated as part of the services by the operator. The last date of submission was March 16, 2008. Requests from vehicle manufacturers, namely, Tata and Ashok

Leyland, for extension of deadline for submission were received. The last date for submission was extended till April 7, 2008, and on yet another request, it was further extended till April 29, 2008.

As part of the process, prospective bidders were encouraged to visit Bogota to study the BRT system operations. A total of seven companies visited Bogota in April 2008. The idea was to gain a fair idea of what was expected of a BRTS bus operator.

Responses to RFP

The response to the RFP was not very encouraging as only three companies responded with financial bids.

- Cargo Motors (quoted for TATA-ULF buses only). Cargo Motors are the authorised Sales and Service Dealer for Tata Motors Ltd. (TML). Cargo Motors is one of the largest TML dealers in India and have a large presence all over Gujarat.
- Orix Auto Infrastructure Services Ltd. (quoted for LEYLAND low-floor and semi-low-floor buses). The company operated Radio Taxi services in various cities.
- Pankaj Gandhi (Chartered Logistics) (quoted for TATA low-floor buses) was the only bidder who had visited Bogota. Chartered Logistics is a cargo logistics service provider with over 2000 trucks.

Comparative bids (charges per kilometre of bus operations), as quoted by the three bidders, are presented in Table 5.4 (Ahmedabad Janmarg Ltd., 2008).

Table 5.4: Rate per bus kilometre (in Rs.)

Sl. No.	**Description**	**Cargo**	**Pankaj Gandhi**	**ORIX**
1	Low floor bus non-air-conditioned	72	63	65.08
2	Low floor bus air-conditioned	81	72	68.60
Bus manufacturer		Tata	Tata	Leyland

Note: Orix quoted prices for each year of the operations period. For comparative assessment, average price has been taken.

Source: AJL tender document.

5.3.2.2 *Analysis*

The project planners did not see the responses received as encouraging. The quoted prices were much above the expected level. Following were some of the concerns of the project designers:

- The manufacturers repeatedly requested for extension of the bid date so that they could give price quotes including Annual Maintenance Contract (AMC) for the term of the operations contract. This was repeatedly mentioned in all the meetings arranged by Janmarg with the various operators.
- The number of bids received was fewer than expected. Most operators who had submitted an Expression of Interest (EoI) could not submit a bid for lack of price quotes from the bus manufacturers. Hence, the bids were not treated as competitive.
- After having delayed the tender process for so long, Tata Motors gave a price quote only to its dealers. Tata Motors' policy of restricting the quotes to select operators was not disclosed in any of the meetings with Janmarg till the last minute.
- Ashok Leyland gave prices only on the day of bid opening.

Based on the experience, it was decided to scrap the bid.

5.3.3 ***The Choice of BRT Bus and the Bus Operator: Second Effort***

As a result of the failed bid process, the project planners were pushed back to the drawing board once again. To ensure a fair and competitive bid process, it was felt that bus specifications in the RFP needed to be broad based. The bus floor height and the fuel option of CNG were considered to be the main limiting factors. A new round of the RFP process was initiated, which included CNG and diesel fuel options, low, semi-low and standard floor height bus options as well as AC and non-AC options.

5.3.3.1 *Revised specifications*

The principal elements of the new tender were:

- Bids were invited for buses with low, semi-low and standard floor height (380 mm, 650 mm, and 860 mm with acceptable deviation levels). High floor was not considered as an appropriate option both from the operations and quality perspectives.

- High standards were maintained in specifications of the coach to ensure quality and create an attractive image. Elements such as automatic doors, air suspension, high quality body and interiors were asked for.
- Bidders could bid for both CNG and/or diesel, but these needed to comply with BS-III (Euro-III) emissions standards.
- Both air-conditioned as well as non-air-conditioned bus options were included (earlier AC buses were the only option).
- Minimum power of the engine was kept as 180 hp.
- The term of the contract was to be seven years.

RFP with the revised and broad-based specifications was issued by Ahmedabad Janmarg Ltd. (AJL) on May 22, 2008. The results are analysed here.

5.3.3.2 *New RFP outcomes*

Five companies responded with their bids. The financial bids were opened on June 26, 2008 and the summary of these is presented in Table 5.5 (Ahmedabad Janmarg Ltd., 2009).

Table 5.5: New RFP outcomes—rate per bus km (in Rs.)

	GSEC-Punjab Travels	**Maruti Travels**	**Pankaj Gandhi 1**	**Pankaj Gandhi 2**	**Lahar Associates**
Design Option A 390–400 mm					
AC	73	66	62.1	54	Nil
Non-AC	64	58	54	48.6	Nil
Average	68.5	62	58.05	51.3	Nil
Fuel Type	Tata CNG	Tata Diesel	Tata CNG	Tata Diesel	
Design Option B 650mm					
AC	69	52	51.3	40.5	59.4
Non-AC	62	46	46.8	36	52.2
Average	65.5	49	49.05	38.25	55.8
Fuel Type	Leyland CNG	Tata Diesel	Leyland CNG	Tata Diesel	Leyland/ Tata Diesel

(*Contd.*)

	GSEC-Punjab Travels	Maruti Travels	Pankaj Gandhi 1	Pankaj Gandhi 2	Lahar Associates
Design Option C 860mm					
AC	Nil	46	Nil	38.7	58.5
Non-AC	Nil	41	Nil	34.2	51.3
Average	Nil	43.5	Nil	36.45	54.9
Fuel Type		Leyland diesel		Leyland diesel	Leyland diesel

Source: AJL Tender Evaluation Report.

The observations below are worth noting:

- Not all potential operators quoted for all possible combinations. Of the possible combinations of bids (floor-height, fuel and AC/Non-AC), 16 bids were available for diesel buses while there were only eight for CNG buses. This indicated the preference of potential operators for a diesel bus. No bidder proposed standard floor height bus with CNG.
- The price bids for low-floor buses were lower than the quotes received in the previous bids.
- The price bids varied significantly across operators. This was perhaps due to varied expectations about the BRT operations. It could also be due to the inability of operators to estimate operations cost (as these bus types were new to the market). In fact, all the bidders were encouraged to visit Bogota and other BRT systems in Latin America to understand what BRT operations meant and entailed.
- Per kilometre prices of an operator also varied significantly across different models of buses. The price for low-floor AC bus was the highest and for the standard floor non-AC bus, it was the lowest. It was difficult to explain why low and semi-low floor buses should cost more! It appears that the product development costs must have been loaded on to the initial lot of buses despite the mass production advantage.
- The prices quoted for the standard floor buses were much lower even when compared to semi-low floor buses. The bids suggested that the standard floor bus was the most economical option for BRTS in Ahmedabad.

5.3.3.3 *The choice of bus*

The price quoted for the operation of a non-AC standard floor height bus was Rs.34.20 per km, and for a similar AC bus it was Rs. 38.70. As against this, the lowest price quoted for the CNG option was Rs. 46.80 for a semi-low-floor, non-AC, CNG bus. There was thus a net difference of Rs. 12.60 per km between the two quotes. At the time of the tender, the earnings per km on the AMTS services were under Rs.18. AJL, from its extensive studies on demand, found that the maximum revenue it could generate from fare collection was Rs. 23 per bus km operated. This, too, would be possible only after major rationalisation of the public transit services. Yet, there would be a net deficit of Rs.11.20 per km in earnings in the case of the first option (standard floor diesel bus) and Rs.23.80 per km in the case of the semi-low-floor CNG option. Hence, the economic advantage was obviously in favour of a standard floor diesel bus.

However, the committee appointed by the Supreme Court to monitor the city's air quality questioned Ahmedabad's decision to power its BRT buses through diesel. The project planners (AJL) prepared a detailed note explaining the circumstances under which the decision was being made, and how it would complement the effort of the committee to reduce the pollutants from transport by attracting more passengers.

The following arguments of AJL in favour of the diesel bus are extracted from its communications to the Committee.

- Generally, experts opine that CNG is a cleaner fuel than diesel and hence it should be chosen as a fuel option. But rather than looking at emissions on a per vehicle basis, it is important that the city look at overall emissions impact. Public transit can bring down the emissions impact substantially. If the city can bring down the mode share of private modes and shift passenger trips on to public transit through a high quality of service, which is possible with the Bus Rapid Transit Service, the shifts from private modes to a cleaner public transit would substantially reduce the impact of emissions on the city's atmosphere. The emissions on a per citizen basis would drop substantially.
- For a total of 200 buses that the city planned to operate as part of BRT at the end of Phase 1 & 2, the total burden on the city would be Rs. 34.27 crore per annum if the CNG option was to

be chosen. This is substantially more than in the case of the first option where the deficit was Rs. 16.12 crore per annum. As a percentage of operating cost subsidies to be given to AJL by the AMC, the CNG option would amount to 51 per cent. The additional burden per annum would amount to Rs.18.15 crore per annum if the fleet size of 200 buses was to be deployed.

- Since the resources of Ahmedabad Municipal Corporation are limited, the city would be forced to reduce the total fleet size from 200 (as planned) to 94 buses if the quantum of subsidy was to be the same (Rs.16.12 crore per annum). This would reduce the services substantially and AJL would not be in a position to provide the quality and frequency of BRT services that it had set out to offer.
- As many as 1,50,000 potential passengers/day on the BRT system would be forced to use private modes of transport or depend on a large fleet of shared auto-rickshaws/Informal Public Transit Services. In such a case, the emissions impact on the city's atmosphere shall be very high.
- It is, therefore, requested that AJL be allowed to bring in 'cheaper cost per km' buses as long as the Euro III emission standards, as mandated, are met with. AJL agrees to do a 100 per cent pollution check of all the vehicles on a monthly basis to make sure that the citizens of Ahmedabad breathe clean air.

The Committee, in response, exempted AJL from the application of the CNG mandate. With this, a diesel-powered, standard floor height bus came into being as the Janmarg bus. This standard floor height also became the BRT 'standard' as it was later included in the Urban Bus Specifications by the Ministry of Urban Development.

5.4 Discussion and Summary

In most developmental projects, there is no one correct way of doing things. Multiple actors are at play and successful implementation would mean successful formation of the actor-network wherein decisions emerge through a collective process.

It is interesting to note that a decade before Janmarg came into being, the development of BRTS system in Bogota too had faced similar controversies with regard to fuel choice, door location as well as floor height. Valderrama (2008: 208) explaining the Transmilenio's decision in favour of high floor buses, concluded that the 'agency was distributed during the process of design and implementation to various parts of the new systems;' the features of the system 'were not only influenced by contingent activities of the planners, designers and politicians involved, but were also related to previous practices;' 'the emphasis placed by designers on making the new system different from the existing ones' and the agency 'was dependent on how the material scripts perform in relations to other elements'(Akrich M., 1992). Janmarg design and development process substantiated the above, as demonstrated in this chapter. The following discussion elaborates some of this, taking the Janmarg context into account and concludes the chapter.

Ahmedabad designed several innovations in the process of building the BRTS. While attempting these, the system also deviated from the generally accepted practice and established a new way of mobility management through the design of technological artifacts and operational tactics.

An important artifact has been the design of a 900 mm standard-floor bus. Contrary to general movement in the industry and regulatory systems that were trying to bring floor height closer to ground with a view to make it more accessible, Ahmedabad decided to adopt a higher floor height. By doing so, a controversy of sorts was raised which was not just limited to floor height. Ahmedabad also introduced doors on the right side for the first time in India, which was not allowed by the Motor Vehicles Act. Choosing diesel as fuel, despite the Supreme Court committee's insistence on CNG was another controversy which the city (project planners) had raised. There were several actors who were performing the action. Multiple actors with varied interests acted in the Janmarg project to arrive at a collaborative design process.

- The project designers (AMC, CEPT, AJL) were interested in sustainable mobility and proposed BRTS as an integral part of the transit system. By introducing BRTS and development of other systems, their objective was to maximise transit ridership so that the city continues to be accessible. While environmental quality was definitely high on the agenda of the project planners, they did not stay with CNG as the only fuel. They focused on the much broader objective of developing quality transit and the economics of running it while keeping in mind the air quality of the city.

- The focus of the monitoring committee appointed by the Supreme Court was on bringing down the air pollution levels, mainly SPM, in the city. Conversion from dirty diesel to CNG was a solution which could yield quick results. There were arguments against the blanket order for conversion of vehicles to CNG. Although the comparative economics of the two fuels was not in favour of CNG, following the precautionary principle, the committee mandated CNG as the fuel for all buses and auto-rickshaws registered in the city.
- Vehicle manufacturers were few in number and had been enjoying a sort of monopoly over the market for a long time. While they focused on perpetuating their leadership in the market, they were not interested in innovations as it would be an expensive option. Their interest was to promote the products that they already had on their shelves.
- For potential bus operators, this was a new window of opportunity, which they wanted to exploit. They understood the risk in such emerging businesses. Attempts to mitigate risks were but natural. Their way of avoiding risk was to prefer technologies that were economical and with which they were familiar. This was demonstrated in their choice of the standard floor height (900 mm) bus which, though new, was closest to the technology familiar to them.
- As noted by one of the bidders, Pankaj Gandhi, while deciding on the price, the bidders have to consider advantages and the likely responses of different stakeholders. "In our view, at the time of the bid, CNG buses had not matured enough for us to consider them favourably. Major disadvantages of the CNG bus, from our perceptive, was its higher capital cost (low floor CNG bus @ Rs. 65-70 lakh/bus), increased gross weight, low mileage, high maintenance costs due to more expensive spare parts and a dearth of skilled technicians, higher fuelling time and higher bus breakdown rate." Quoting experiences of the AMTS and the DTC, he said that the operators feared that CNG buses were more prone to fire risks than diesel buses. Explaining their bid decisions, Pankaj Gandhi stated that while they bid for all technically feasible options, while deciding on the price, they

took into account the additional risks of CNG-powered buses. In the absence of CNG-powered engines meeting the tender specification of 180+ hp, they did not bid for standard floor height CNG buses (Gandhi, 2015).

- Mr. Lakra, an automobile expert, justified the assessment of the bidders as: "ICEs using diesel fuels are easy to operate, maintain and repair as spares and skills required are readily available in the country. In contrast, CNG vehicles have a higher total system weight, reduced power, high operating and maintenance costs, and higher initial capital costs. These vehicles also require additional fuelling infrastructure which adds to the capital costs. Hence private operators are expected to load the risk of operating CNG on to the public sector through a relatively higher price bid" (Lakra, 2015).
- Non-human factors, namely, the fuel as well as the floor height, had their role to perform. CNG did not cooperate with standard or semi-low floor buses as it was relatively expensive to build CNG buses with that floor height. So also the floor height, which limited the location of the engine as well as the fuel tank. The rough, pot-holed, winding and narrow roads in India also did not cooperate with the low floor buses.

Given the large number of actors involved in the process, the design decision of the BRT bus for Ahmedabad did not rest with any single actor. The bus design evolved through the distribution of agency across various actors. Market provided a common platform through which the network of actors could arrive at the design decisions.

As presented above, the features of the bus were not decided independently of each other. The bus-floor height decision influenced the location of the engine, its power, fuel choice as well as the door location. As noted by Valderrama and Jorgensen, the "features were not only influenced by contingent activities of the planners, designers and politicians involved, but were also related to previous practices" (Valderrama & Jorgensen, 2008: 208).

Ahmedabad BRTS project planners needed to discontinue the existing practices and conventions so that the new system could be protected from the existing. The design of doors on the right side was a critical decision in making the new different from the existing. This has been discussed in detail in the previous chapter.

It is to be noted that although the Ahmedabad BRTS project planners deviated from the existing practices and conventions, they did not compromise on the core objectives. The advantage is that this bus, with high platform bus stations (discussed in Chapter 4) enables level boarding as well as passenger movement control. Further, the flat floor inside the bus enables efficient movement. The two wide doors of the bus on the right side, introduced for the first time in India, enables operational control of the BRTS. With electronically enabled docking of doors (both of the bus and the bus station), controlled by the driver, and the bus being able to move only when the doors close, is one of the unique contributions of the BRTS of Ahmedabad to transit development. As the system became popular, mode shifts from auto-rickshaws and two-wheelers occurred. As noted in the monthly reports prepared by CEPT — Centre of Excellence in Urban Transport, nearly half of the BRTS riders had not been using the bus service before the start of BRTS (CoE-UT, CEPT University, 2014). These shifts imply reduction in pollution emission loads.

This goes to prove that though discontinuity from the 'old' is necessary to protect and promote the 'new', continuity (building on the existing but still making it different) from the 'old' in certain core elements makes the 'new' get established (and overtake the old) quickly. This was observed in the choice of standard floor diesel bus as opposed to CNG. From the operators' perspective, the engine, tyres, tubes, fuel and several other components in the new bus were also part of the old bus, which they had operated and maintained for a long time. The only major change in the new bus was the reduction of floor height through the design of an out-triggered coach. Of course, improvements in terms of ITS applications, multiplexing, adoption of BS-IV etc., were made in the bus with the passage of time. Thus, it may be stated that both continuity and discontinuity are two essential parts of the new bus. The right decisions about what is to be discontinued and what is to be continued appears to make or break the success of the innovation.

With regard to CNG application, with the introduction of BS-IV emission norms, the emphasis on CNG appears to have been watered down. The AMTS has now moved to diesel buses (BS-IV) again for similar reasons. It appears that the adoption of CNG on the basis of the 'precautionary principle' could only be ensured if mandated. It could have been made into a successful option if the market had been moulded such that choice of CNG became economically viable.

NOTES

1. In addition, vehicle design has to be matched with the characteristics of the other elements of the system, including running ways, bus station design, service plans, intelligent transport system (ITS) application and fare collection. This aspect has been dealt with in detail in the previous chapter.
2. Enquiries with international bus manufacturers suggested the following prices. The price of an imported 12 metre bus would have been in the order of 1.5 to 2.0 crore as opposed Rs. 40 to 60 lakh for a bus manufactured in India (without considering differences in quality, life of the bus etc.). Similarly, articulated buses cost about Rs. 3 to 3.5 crore each.
3. The first prototype of an articulated bus manufactured in India was displayed in the year 2014 and it is stated to be made available for operations in 2017. In 2014, Ahmedabad city has also ordered two such buses for operation on pilot basis.
4. Presentation made to the Supreme Court Committee on the issue of CNG versus Diesel in May 2008 (AMC, CoE-UT CEPT University, 2008).
5. PHPDT is derived for no passing lane infrastructure with open junction limiting one minute headway.
6. Sulfur content in diesel improved with successive introduction of emission norms. BS-II introduced in 2001 was 500 ppm, BS-III introduced in 2005 was 350 ppm and BS-IV introduced in 2010 is 50 ppm.
7. Author's own assessment.

6
Epilogue

6.1 Overview

The focus of this publication is to understand the process of large-scale transport project development, taking Ahmedabad BRTS — from conceptualisation to commissioning and beyond — as a case study, by using the three key concepts of ANT: translation — to explain the project development process; artifacts and their inscriptions — designing artifacts to influence user behaviour, and to make network durable; and, delegation and distribution of agency — to illustrate how decisions emerge out of actor-network interactions rather than emanating out of an actor. The findings of the study have been summarised in three parts.

6.2 Translation

Is the Ahmedabad BRTS a success?

A successful project manages to convince more people to support its aims, even as it manages to involve more institutions in funding. It also mobilises experts in implementation, and makes greater use of material objects that give the project a more durable physical form.

The focal actors in Ahmedabad were able to successfully translate the competitors into collaborators. Also they were successful in winning over large sections of society, politicians and the project affected people. In this process, the designers were able to design artifacts which help shape human behaviour. It was also realised that decisions emerge out of the negotiations within the network and not by any single actor. The physical manifestation through various artifacts of over 80 km implies that, at the current stage, the project is durable, irreversible and hence may be termed as successful.

The BRTS project in Ahmedabad, as analysed in Chapter 3, went through phases of challenges. The construction began in 2007 and the system was opened for commercial operations in 2009. The network expanded within a short duration of time. The actors, both human and non-human, contributed towards development of a high quality service. Ridership grew with increase in the network. By 2011, daily average ridership with 45 kms of network in operation had increased to 1,40,000-1,50,000. Monthly customer reviews showed high system ratings (score of 8.5 out of 10). Awards — national and international — were conferred to the system, recognising it as a 'best mass transit project,' suggesting the success of the project.

However, the translations overtime were dynamic. The original design underwent several changes. It continues to undergo changes even in areas where the system elements are supposedly completely built and commercial operations are underway.

This project showed that success is dynamic through the lifecycle. Several actors, with changed interests, decided not to cooperate with the BRTS. Expansion of the network involved several compromises in design due to change in legislations related to heritage structures, among others. The city bus operator AMTS continued to operate its services on the BRT network. Metro planners decided to select a network which competed with the BRTS network. On-street parking restrictions could not be enforced, which led to reduction in road space for mixed traffic. Other vehicles started entering the BRTS corridor. As the network expanded from 45 km to 80 km by 2013, the bus fleet increase was slow. As a result, BRTS services were operating with reduced frequency. Despite the increase in the network, the average daily ridership remained stagnant at 140,000.

The above discussion points out two important conclusions. The first is that success or failure is not a permanent state. In fact, it is only at a point in time during the project life cycle, and projects go through several ups and downs. The second is that there are no clear answers as to what causes success or failure. It is also evident that if the network is formed, as in this case BRTS project, it means that all the actors are agreeing to align their interests with that of the project. This is the state which one may call as success. However, failure to hold the actors together, for example when AMTS, existence of heritage monuments etc., decided not to cooperate, led to reopening of the black boxes.

To solicit support from other actors, focal actors tend to widen the scope. In the case of Ahmedabad BRTS, the project was structured as an integrated transit project and a large network for BRTS development was identified as a strategy. Wide scope also meant inviting interference from the actors. In the case of Ahmedabad, this worked both ways. In the first phase, widened scope brought acceptance from commuters, elected representatives, metro rail system, AMTS etc., as the defined problem did not compete with their own interest. But with the expansion of the network, conflict of interest among the actors (for instance, AMTS) surfaced, and as a result, interests of some actors (AMTS and Metro) changed resulting in re-opening of the black box. In both cases, the existing and potential saw BRTS as a threat to their existence or their coming into being and hence revolted. Efforts to convert competitors into collaborators only succeeded partially and for some time. Failure to implement integrated service and fare to travel on multiple modes only added to the problem. However, the efforts to make the system work as an integrated unit are again being initiated. The findings are that while broad based definition of the problem will be attractive to some, in the long run, the differences amongst the actors which were not visible initially may surface prominently, weakening the bonding of actors within the network.

In this case, the interests of the competitors, viz. AMTS, metro rail system and shared auto-rickshaw were translated by the focal actors by defining broadly the OPP as 'Integrated Transit' and was successful in convincing others that everyone's interest is in achieving this objective. However, with time, their contexts change and so also do their interests. Latour's (1987) notion of 'science and technology in the making' is substantiated by the project development process studied here. The project defined in 2006 as part of DPR, had to undergo (and is still undergoing) a series of changes in its design and operating systems. These are mainly necessitated to accommodate the interests of or to overcome negotiation process with other emerging actors. To illustrate a few: the network of corridors had to undergo change, the alignment of a bridge was changed, the design of streets had to undergo several changes due to existence of religious structures and encroachments. Station access design was also changed several times. Fare collection system had to be changed thrice. These changes are due to non-cooperation of certain actors, failed contracts or to accommodate interests of some actors. As noted by Swamy (2014), the

BRTS planning and design is not a one-time activity but a continuous process. Thus planning, design, development and operations are simultaneous yet continuous processes.

As stated above, in the case of Ahmedabad, this study shows that there are multiple networks functioning simultaneously. Even a single focal actor (in this case, the AMC or Ahmedabad Municipal Corporation) is attempting to build multiple networks towards its goal of enhancing the BRTS. It is also possible that depending on the actors in the network, the definition of OPP may differ. However, OPPs of a project cannot be conflicting with each other. For instance, when attempting to overcome competition with other transit providers, the OPP defined is 'integrated transit'. On the other hand, while attempting to manage interference from the users, non-users, streets etc., the focal actors defined OPP as 'Complete Network — Complete Streets'. In both, the effort has been to accommodate others' interests to the extent possible even while attempting to win over the competitors and resistors through an accommodative approach. In both the cases, the OPP was a broader goal towards which all actors had to work.

It is to be noted that in the development process, the focal actors have also shifted. The project was initiated by GIDB, an agency created to promote private sector investment in public infrastructure development. With the opportunity of funds from JnNURM (Jawaharlal Nehru National Urban Renewal Mission), GIDB withdrew its role as focal actor (though informally) and the AMC took it over. It also made sense because implementation was anyway going to be the responsibility of the AMC. It is important to note that in a large initiative, the focal actors may not remain the same. The success of projects and their long term stability also depends on how a network evolves.

In fact, sometimes in the project cycle, another shift in the focal actor appeared imminent. The Metro, with its large financial resource pool, has put integration of transit modes including last mile connectivity as part of its approved DPR. This would mean emergence of a new actor-network. Recently, the Ministry of Urban Development (MoUD) has initiated a study to examine the institutionalisation of the Unified Metropolitan Transit Authority, which will have the mandate to ensure that multi-modal integrated transit systems operate in cities. It is to be seen as how these networks develop and how the various actors and their roles get re-defined.

6.3 Designing Artifacts to Shape Human Behaviour

In an attempt to make actor-networks durable, the designers built several artifacts and inscribed their programmes of action.

There exist multiple artifacts and their programmes of action. There are several artifacts that designers built as part of BRTS in Ahmedabad. They included corridors and various elements such as stations and its components, fare collection systems, control centre, intelligent transport systems, AJL, operating systems etc. The primary programme of action behind design of these is to provide a protective envelope to BRTS so that it can operate with desired functionality and long-term stability. In fact, it is possible to draw parallels between how BRTS designers attempted to control the operating environment through use of artifacts, intelligent transport systems and trained workforce.

Multiple scripts were developed for a single programme of action. They were inscribed in a single artifact and a single artifact was inscribed with multiple scripts. For example, the script 'only BRTS buses' accompanies the police notification, BRTS station, buses, bus operator contract, as well as the traffic signal. Similarly, the script 'stop at bus stations only' is inscribed into ITS, bus door, bus station door, door control system using GPRS tag, bus etc. The strategy with the use of multiple artifacts and multiple scripts is to make inscription stronger by reinforcing it with one another. This is important for bringing stability to the network.

It is assumed that stronger the inscription, more stable will be the network. Inscriptions in some cases are inscribed into the artifact, while others accompany the artifact. The former is relatively stronger. For instance, the script 'bus only' for the corridors inscribed using police commissioner notification, allows for fine as well as impounding of vehicles other than BRTS buses if they enter the corridor. But this is not enforceable as the powers to impound the vehicles are given only to the traffic police. The strength of the police force deployed for this is so minimal that enforcement is difficult. Secondly, given the vast network and the tendency of personalised vehicle users to enter the BRTS lanes, taking the impounded vehicle to storage and then to the court is a major task making it impractical to manage this aspect. Instead, a reasonable level of fine and the delegation of the power to fine to the BRTS security personnel would have been more effective.

The point is: how strong the inscriptions should be, depends on the requirement of the situation.

But it is not always the programme of action and the scripts of the designers which are followed (inscribed). The users and the artifacts also inscribe their own scripts by following their own programme of action (anti-programme). For example, in Ahmedabad BRTS, in order to provide wheelchair access to bus stations, bollards spacing was appropriately provided. The two-wheeler users saw this as an opportunity to cross over and started using it to take 'U-turns'. This became unsafe and hence designers changed the design to provide wheelchair access on the opposite side. This again could not prevent the two wheeler users to use this for taking a U-turn. Finally the designers had to reduce the gap such that two-wheelers cannot enter the corridor. This also meant wheelchair access to the stations was blocked on one side of all stations.

This case highlights the role of user and technology (artifact) as designers. It also brings the politics of technology to the fore. One of the prime objectives of BRTS development is to provide universal accessibility. This effort was underway around the same time when the national government was also trying to make buses accessible by lowering the floor height. Contrary to this, Ahmedabad BRTS designers designed a high floor bus, raised platforms of the bus stations, and arranged secured level boarding with ITS interface. This, in fact, provided better access to the wheelchair users. However, the change made in bollard spacing, limited station accessibility at a few stations.

6.4 Distribution of Agency

As noted earlier, according to the Actor-Network Theory, agency is not an a priori feature of an actor but is an outcome of interactions between the heterogeneous actors in the network. The notion of 'distributed agency' emphasises that agency is not located in an individual actor but is distributed among diverse (human and non-human) actors that jointly form a collective (Gomart & Hennion, 1999) as cited in Harbers, 2005: 86). Chapter 5 provided insights into this concept.

There were decisions to be made regarding bus design, fuel, station, station access etc., and there were multiple actors involved in the decision. These included the AMC, the CEPT, the Supreme Court Committee, the MoUD, the operators, the manufacturers and the relevant non-human actors. Each of the choices available had their own merit from the perspective of some actors. For instance, the Supreme Court Committee recommended a CNG-powered bus considering environmental impacts. The operators wanted diesel bus because of familiarity with technology and ease of maintenance. The AMC, though neutral to fuel, was concerned about the cost of operations. CEPT was concerned about the appropriate level of power and functionality. Manufacturers not willing to innovate were interested in selling technology that they already had. Thus, the entire decision process was complex and riddled with uncertainties. No clear choice seemed to be emerging. The decision was sorted out by using a market mechanism which led to purchase of diesel fuelled high-floor buses.

The 900 mm floor height bus, designed and adopted by Janmarg, has now become a standard for BRT systems in India.[1] Most of the city-BRT projects[2] being developed in India have adopted the 900 mm floor-height, diesel-powered, right-side-door bus as their vehicle of choice. The Urban Bus Specifications mandated by the MoUD, Government of India, adopted the 900 mm floor-height bus as the standard BRT bus floor height. Further, it is worth noting that the bus designed as the BRT bus is the most popular model among all floor height buses, and is widely applied in mixed traffic operations as well.

This goes to prove that though discontinuity from the 'old' is necessary to protect and promote the 'new'. However, in urban areas which are already developed, erasing the old and bringing in the new may not be possible. This was observed in the choice of standard floor diesel bus as opposed to a CNG one. From the operators' perspective, the engine, tyres, tubes, fuel and several other components in the new bus were also part of the old bus, which they had operated and maintained for a long time. The only major change in the new bus was the reduction of floor height through design of an out-triggered coach. Of course, improvements in terms of ITS applications, multiplexing, adoption of BS-IV etc., were also made in the bus over time. The right decisions about what is to be discontinued and what is to be continued appear to contribute to the success of the innovation.

6.5 Conclusion

The discussion in this book has brought out several important facets of urban planning,especially those related to transport and the use of the

ANT framework in large-scale transport project development. Some of the important findings are:

(a) The translations were found to be dynamic.
(b) It confirms the findings of earlier studies that success or failure is not a permanent state. In fact, it is only a point of time during the project life cycle. Secondly, at some points, all the actors seem to agree to align their interests with that of the project. This shows the state of success, even though it failed to hold other actors together. In a classical sense, the actors do not cooperate leading to reopening of the black boxes. This is clearly an addition to the literature which would be useful for several infrastructure projects that are being set up by India in particular and the developing countries in general.
(c) Another important addition to the literature is the finding that the agency is not an a priori feature of an actor but is an outcome of interactions between the heterogeneous actors in the network. The notion of 'distributed agency' emphasises that agency is not located in an individual actor but is distributed among diverse (human and non-human) actors that jointly form a collective.

It is well recognised that there are very few studies on urban infrastructure provisioning,especially in the Indian context. In this perspective, this study makes an important contribution to not only the literature but also to scholars and implementers alike. It also highlights the need for documentation of the features of large public infrastructure implementation, especially in the urban context.

As stated earlier, project development is a continuous process. The BRT system in Ahmedabad has evolved over time and continues to evolve. The development projects such as BRTS, planning, design, development and operations are not sequential stages of development but are simultaneous and dynamic in nature.

This raises a question on the project development processes and assessment processes adopted so far. Most agencies tend to follow a sequence of activities such as preparation of project note, pre-feasibility study followed by a feasibility study, environmental and social assessment, approval, detailed design, procurement, implementation, monitoring and evaluation. Often, it is observed that the project development stage takes about three to four years. In the light of the findings of this study, this sequential approach toward a developmental project does not seem to reflect the reality. Therefore, further research to review and restructure the project assessment practices is required.

NOTES

1. Of the total 16,939 buses sold with JnNURM funding in India during the past 10 years, 47 per cent of the buses were of 900 mm floor height model, followed by 20.48 per cent — 400 mm model, 12.9 per cent-650 mm and 15.3 per cent of mini and midi buses.
2. The systems developed in Pune, Surat, Rajkot, Indore, Amritsar, Hubli-Dharwad, Amritsar have all adopted the bus similar to the Ahmedabad Janmarg bus.

APPENDICES

Appendix 1

Bus Rapid Transit System

Introduction

Till recently, the world had limited options for public transport. In cities it was confined to low-end bus system, tram modernised subsequently as light rail transit (LRT), and metro till the idea of Bus Rapid Transit System (BRTS) was born in Curitiba, Brazil, in 1974 (Grossman, n.d.). The concept was taken forward by integrating transit and land use development in the plan for development of the city. In 1998, the Colombian city of Bogota chose the construction of a BRTS over a metro rail system. Although the performance of the BRTS in terms of capacity and quality matched that of the metro rail system, its capital cost was much lower, thus making it a viable low-cost sustainable rapid transit option for the city. Many Latin American cities followed suit and successfully implemented BRT systems to cater to their growing mobility demand.

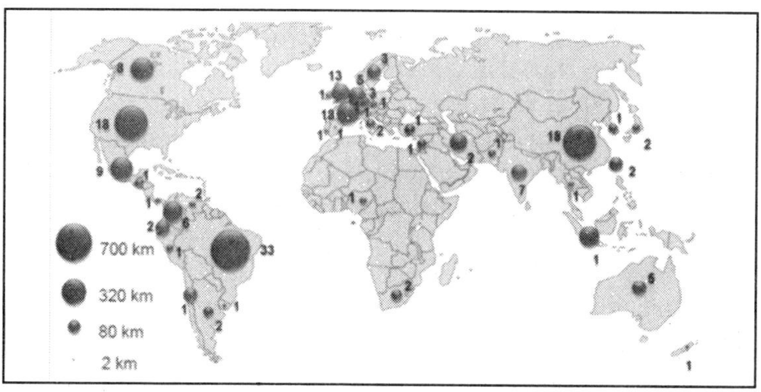

Source: Global BRT Data (2015).

Fig. A-1: BRTS operational across the world

This note presents a comparative picture of various mass rapid transit systems.

Generally five types of urban mass rapid transit systems, four rail-based and one bus-based, are identified as MRT systems. They are Metro Rail, Light Rail Transit, Monorail, Suburban Rail, and Bus Rapid Transit System. Though suburban rail is also a mass rapid transit system, as it is generally a part of the larger regional rail network and provides connects the city with its hinterland, it is not included for discussion in this section.

Metro rail system

Metro rail is a high-capacity, high-cost system with fully segregated right-of-way. The RoW is mostly elevated or underground and sometimes at-grade. The first Metro line of the world was built in 1863 in London (Metrobits, 2016). Over the years, several cities have adopted metro rail system as a rapid transit option. Today, globally, 195 cities have operational metro rail systems with a combined network length of 11,936 km, and carry on an average 112 million passengers each day. (Metrobits, 2014-2015)

As stated above, most important features of the metro rail system are its high carrying capacity and high speed. Its highest known carrying capacity is 90,000 PHPDT as observed in Tokyo and Beijing. Travel speeds range between 30 km/h and 40 km/h. While there is an emphasis on the maximum carrying capacity, not much focus is given to the minimum thresholds (Swamy *et. al.*, 2015: 195). If the demand is low, the operating expenses tend to be prohibitive. The capital cost of the systems vary from INR 200 crore per kilometre in case of elevated Metro to INR 500 crore per kilometre for an underground Metro. Metro is energy efficient and a safe rapid transit option. Despite the high costs and high threshold demand level, most cities tend to consider developing metro as part of their mass transit system option.

Monorail

Monorail vehicles either ride on or are suspended from a single rail or a beam (Vuchik, 2007, p. 578). The first Monorail was opened in Wuppertal, Germany, in 1901. Despite the long history, there are only 26 monorail urban applications found and these are limited to short distances. Though the monorail companies have been proactive in marketing, cities tend to get discouraged due to their high capital costs (INR 130 crore per kilometre) (Swamy *et. al.*, 2015: 196). Further, technology is vendor-specific. However, Monorail's small volume and compact structure makes it appropriate for application in complex terrain conditions and narrow streets.

Tram/streetcar/light rail transit (LRT)

Trams and their modern version, LRT, have been the most popular urban mass transit option for cities. They were popular in the late 19th and early 20th century, but many cities abandoned them in the post-war period of rapid growth in private-vehicle ownership. During the last three or four decades, renewed interest in bringing back the streetcar as an LRT system has been observed. Today the tram/LRT exists in 374 cities around the world, with a total network of 17,000 km. The observed speed ranges between 18 km/h and 24 km/h. The capital cost of setting up an LRT system is estimated at INR 70-90 crore per kilometre. There was a proposal to build LRT in Delhi.

BRTS

BRT is often defined to consist of elements which are bundled together to operate as a system. These are: transit network, running ways, stations, vehicles, fare collection, intelligent transportation system, service and operation plan, and branding and communications. Each of these can be configured differently to determine the system's performance.

Transit Network: BRTS can be implemented as one or more corridors or a complete network

Running Ways: Running ways in which BRT buses ply can be designed as elevated or at-grade with different levels of segregation. In terms of placement, the BRT lanes may be developed on the kerb side of the carriageway, or as median lanes running in the centre of the roadway.

Stations and Terminals: Stations and Terminals are the interface between commuters and the system. They provide support at three levels, namely, passenger facility, operations and management. For commuters this infrastructure provides easy transfers, safe and comfortable environment in the transit zone and easy exchange of transit information. The terminal, at high demand locations, acts as a node with multiple services, some services terminating and others passing through and providing safe interchange opportunity.

Buses: A 'bus' is an elementary component of the BRTS. These vehicles have a strong effect on every measurable aspect of system performance. Vehicle design plays a vital role in addressing system capacity, speed, convenience, operational revenue as well as economic concerns. Buses are the identity of the system for the commuters.

Fare Collection: Fare is the fee paid by passengers for transit services provided by the operator against the operational cost of the system. The fares are designed in the local context so as to recover operational cost, which may be designed for partial recovery if the system has sources of non-fare-box revenue or receives external economic benefits. The fare may be collected on-board or off-board; it could be a flat fare, or zonal or distance-based; and may allow intra-system or inter-system interchange, based on the technology in use.

Intelligent Transportation Management Systems (ITMS): The primary aim is to create a system that would allow the regulator, along with the service providers, to manage their activities in a highly coordinated manner leading to better productivity and offering reliable services to the users. The system also aims at creating processes that continually allow the operations to be monitored against accepted service levels, and provide improvement opportunities to transit managers so that they can offer services at best operational levels. It also increases the reliability of the passenger information system for commuters.

Operations, Planning and Management: Full-day service, variable schedules (peak and off-peak), automated scheduling and dispatch system, automated vehicle monitoring and maintenance, and continuous service quality assessments including passenger feedback, are important features of BRTS operations. Service conditions for operators (bus, station and other staff) and their training are critical elements for achieving desirable standard operations.

Branding and Communications: To differentiate the image of BRTS from that of a regular bus transit system, branding and communication strategies are necessary. These may include an attractive name, logo or graphics for the system, dress codes for employees, visiting cards, mementos, newsletters etc. Branding can be made visible on all physical elements such as the bus, bus station, terminals and depots. In addition, communication strategies like interactive information sharing through maps, websites, and other media as well as other forms of public relations exercises contribute to creating a brand image of the system.

According to Global BRT data (2015), there are 194 BRTS across the world (see Fig. A-1), with a total of 5356 km of operational corridors and 32 million riders using the systems every day.

A Comparative Assessment

A comparative assessment of the systems has been presented above. From table below it is evident that although all the systems are designed to carry large numbers of people at a rapid speed, their appropriateness varies with the context within which they are to be applied. Capacity requirements, costs (capital and operating), accessibility levels and land availability are some of the critical determining characteristics.

Table A-1: MRTS: A comparative assessment

Indicators	Metro rail	LRTS	BRTS	Monorail
Type of segregation	Elevated or underground	At-grade with horizontal segregation	At-grade with horizontal segregation (soft or hard)	Elevated
Capacity (PHPDT)	15000-90000	5000-12000	3000-50000	5000-20000
Travel speeds (km/h)	30-40	18-24	20-28 (40)	30
Cost per km (INR crore)	200-500	70-90	12-15	130
Average station spacing	1000-1200 meters	600-800 meters	500-600 meters	1000-1200 meters
Period of implementation (Planning to commissioning)	6-10 years	5-10 years	2-4 years	6-10 years
Land acquisition	Not required except for depots	Re-allocating road space amongst the uses does not require major land acquisition	Re-allocating road space amongst the uses does not require major land acquisition	Not required except for depots

Source: Adapted from Swamy *et al.* 2015: 198) and Vuchic (2007)

Swamy *et al.* (2015) analysed the data from the websites of individual systems to trace the growth of various sub-systems. Their analysis shows that 593 cities in the world have one or more forms of mass rapid transit systems operating there. As Figure 3-1 shows, while trams in their original form and the LRT in the modern form have been the system of choice for long, over a period of time Metro systems have gained ground. And in the past 15 years BRT development has gained momentum.

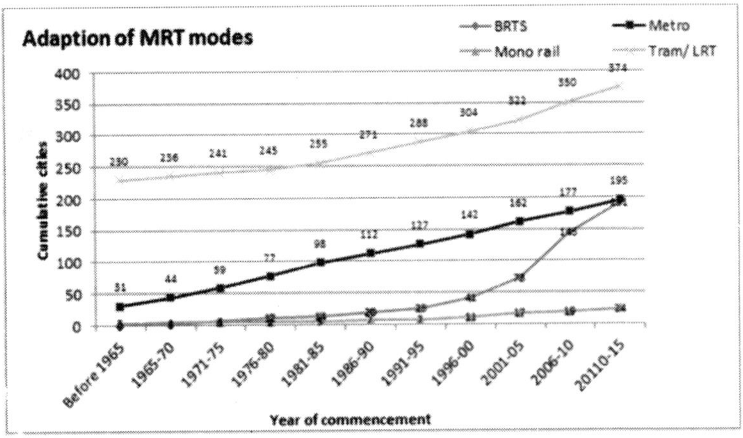

Source: Swamy, et. al., 2015: 200.

Fig. A-2 Adaption of MRT systemsworldwide

Technically speaking, all the MRT systems are distinct in terms of physical, financial, and performance characteristics, and deliver transit services that are distinguishable in quality, quantity and costs.

Appendix 2
Bus Specifications

Specification description	AMTS				BRT Tender 1	BRT Tender 2		
	Standard old (High Floor)	**Standard CNG (High Floor)**	**Mini**	**Semi-Low Floor**	**Low Floor**	**Low Floor**	**Semi-Low Floor**	**Standard Floor**
Floor height (mm)	1100	1060	1000	710	380	380	670	860
Bus length (m)	10.5	10.5	8	11	12	12	11	11
Fuel	Diesel	CNG	CNG	Diesel	CNG	Fuel not specified	Fuel not specified	Fuel not specified
Emissions standard	Euro O	Euro III	Euro II	Euro II	Euro III	Euro III	Euro III	Euro III
Engine capacity (HP)	90	120	72	130	>195	>160	>160	>160
Engine location	Front	Front	Front	Rear	Rear	Rear	Rear	Front

(Contd.)

Specification description	AMTS				BRT Tender 1	BRT Tender 2		
	Standard old (High Floor)	Standard CNG (High Floor)	Mini	Semi-Low Floor	Low Floor	Low Floor	Semi-Low Floor	Standard Floor
Transmission	Manual	Manual	Manual	Manual	Automatic with retarder	Automatic with retarder	Manual	Manual
Steering	Manual	Manual	Manual	Power assist	Power assist	Power assist	Power assist	Power assist
Suspension	Leaf Spring	Leaf Spring	Leaf Spring	Leaf Spring	Full Air	Air / Weveller	Air / Weveller	Air / Weveller
Door type	No	No	No	Manual	Automatic JK type	Automatic JK type	Automatic JK type	Automatic JK type
Number of doors openings	2 × 800 mm	2 × 800 mm	1 × 1000 mm	1 × 1000 mm, 1 × 1300 mm	LH side (2 nos) 1100 mm, RH side (2 nos) 1100 mm	LH side (1 nos) 1400 mm, RH side (2 nos) 1100 mm	LH side (1 nos) 1400 mm, RH side (2 nos) 1100 mm	LH side (1 nos) 1400 mm, RH side (2 nos) 1100 mm
Windows	Al frame	Al frame	Al frame	Al frame with packing	Al frame with Vibration reduction	Al frame with Vibration reduction	Al frame with Vibration reduction	Al frame with Vibration reduction

(*Contd.*)

Specification description	AMTS				BRT Tender 1	BRT Tender 2		
	Standard old (High Floor)	**Standard CNG (High Floor)**	**Mini**	**Semi-Low Floor**	**Low Floor**	**Low Floor**	**Semi-Low Floor**	**Standard Floor**
Outer body paneling	Al sheets	Al + Stretch steel	FRP	Stretch steel	Stretch steel	Al + Stretch steel	Al + Stretch steel	Al + Stretch steel
Flooring	Al checkered sheet	Al checkered sheet	Plywood with Al. strips	Silicon Grain sheet	Silicon Grain sheet	Silicon Grain sheet	Silicon Grain sheet	Silicon Grain sheet
Roof / Side insulation	No	No	No	No	Insulated	Insulated	Insulated	Insulated
Seats	Pipe frame with foam-rexine pad	Pipe frame with foam-rexine pad	Pipe frame with foam-rexine pad	Moulded Plastic with padding	Moulded plastic	Moulded plastic	Moulded plastic	Moulded plastic

Source: Ahmedabad Municipal Corporation, 2008.

Appendix 3
BRTS Project Status Sanctioned Under JnNURM

City	Length (km)	Sanction date	Sanctioned amount (in Rs crore)	Physical progress	Date of completion	Network operational (km)	Remarks
Indore	11.65	11-Aug-06	98.45	Complete	Complete	11.65	Cars allowed on bus lanes after HC directive in September 2013
Bhopal	42.19	10-Nov-06	247.12	85%	Mar-14	16	System inaugurated in September 2013, 6 km BRTS in mixed traffic
Pune	17	11-Aug-06	103.13	Complete	Complete	17	Regional buses allowed on corridor, design being modified on future corridors
	48.77	25-Oct-06	476.62	95%	Mar-14		
	36	05-Mar-07	434.22	94%	Mar-14		
	13.9	19-Aug-08	36.49	Complete	Complete		
Total	115.67		1050.46				
Pimpri Chinchwad	23	28-Dec-07	312.14	70%	Mar-14		
	11.2	21-Nov-08	219.2	34%	Mar-14	11.2	
	7.08	21-Nov-08	206.82	75%	Mar-14		
Total	41.28		738.16				

(Contd.)

City	Length (km)	Sanction date	Sanctioned amount (in Rs crore)	Physical progress	Date of completion	Network operational (km)	Remarks
Ahmedabad	12	11-Aug-06	87.6	Complete	Complete	82	3 km BRTS in mixed traffic
	46	06-Oct-06	405.72	Complete	Complete		
	30.5	19-Aug-08	488.13	72%	Mar-14		
Total	88.5		981.45				
Surat	29.9	07-Mar-08	469.02	55%	Dec-13	10	10 km to be operational by November 2013
Rajkot	29	20-Jul-07	110	Complete	Complete	10.7	Part of the corridor completed with cost escalation
Vijaywada	15.18	26-Mar-07	151	70%	Mar-14		
Vishakhapatnam	45.2	18-May-07	452.93	75%	Mar-14		
Jaipur	39.45	20-Jul-07	75.19	Complete	Complete	7	
		28-Dec-07	144	28%	Mar-14		
		14-Nov-09	260.35	72%	Mar-14		
Total	39.45		479.54				
Amritsar	30	Feb 2014	487				
Total under JnNURM	**488.02**		**5265.13**			**174.35**	

Source: JnNURM, 2013 and CoE-UT, CEPT University, Ahmedabad.

Appendix 4
Ahmedabad BRTS—National and International Recognition

1. Received National Award for "Best Mass Transit Rapid System Project — 2009" under JnNURM scheme on 3rd December, 2009 by Honorable Prime Minister, Government of India.
2. International Award for "Sustainable Transport Award — 2010" at Washington DC, USA on 12th January, 2010.
3. International Award for "Outstanding Innovations in Public Transportation — 2010" from UITP, Germany on 27th May, 2010 by International Transport Forum and International Association of Public Transport.
4. National Award for "Best Innovation Project towards Improvement in Urban Mobility in the City of Ahmedabad through New Technological Innovations in Janmarg BRTS — 2010" from Government of India on 5th December, 2010.
5. The Bus Rapid Transit System (BRTS) of Ahmedabad received an International Award for Design — "Daring Ambition Award and Knowledge and Research Award — 2011" at 59th UITP World Congress, Dubai on 14th April, 2011.
6. National Award for "Award for Excellence in the category of Best ITS Project — 2011" from Ministry of Urban Development, Government of India on 6th December, 2011.
7. "Momentum for Change" an International Award for the category of 2012 Light House Activities to Ahmedabad Bus Rapid Transit System Janmarg by United Nations at Doha on on 5th December, 2012.
8. Ahmedabad Janmarg Limited — AJL has won one award at 60th UITP World Congress, Geneva on 27th May, 2013. AJL-AMC

have received award in the category of "UITP India Political Commitment Award." This award was given by Mr. Peter Hendy, President Elect UITP, in the presence of other UITP delegates from all over the world and delegates from India.

9. AJL has received "MARKENOMY Awards 2013" in the category of "Best Urban Infra Mass Transport Project in India" on 26th September, 2013 organised by Falcon Media, an enterprise of Enertia Foundation at Juhu Club Millennium, Mumbai.
10. Ahmedabad Janmarg Ltd won HUDCO award from Housing & Urban Development Corporation Ltd (HUDCO) in category of Urban Transport on 27th April, 2015 at India Habitat Centre, New Delhi.

Interviewees

1. Mr. A.S. Lakra, former Director, Central Institute of Road Transport, an expert in automobile engineering and consultant to Janmarg (Interview date: 15 May, 2014).
2. Mr. Akhil Bhrambhatt, Dy. General Manager, Janmarg (Interview date: 30 and 31 August, 2013).
3. Mr. Anil Mukim, Former Municipal Commissioner, AMC, from January 2005 to May 2006 (Interview date: 18 November, 2015).
4. Mr. Asit Vora, Former Mayor, and also Former Chairman of Standing Committee and Chairman of the AMTS of the Ahmedabad Municipal Corporation (Interview date: 27 and 28 August, 2015).
5. Mr. C.L. Meena, Former Chairman of the Gujarat Pollution Control Board, which is responsible for regulating environment in the State and was coordinating the efforts of the State in reducing air pollution with the Supreme Court Committee (Interview date: 30 November, 2013).
6. CEPT team (Prof. Shivanand Swamy, Mr. Abhijeet Lokre, Mr. Vijay Arya, Ms. Shalini Sinha and Mr. Chintan Daftardar) (Interview date: At various points in time, individually and as a group).
7. Dr. G.P. Mohapatra (IAS), Municipal Commissioner, AMC Ahmedabad and CMD, Janmarg (Interview date: 10 October, 2015).
8. Mr. Gautam Patel, Finance and PPP expert, Ahmedabad (Interview Date: 14 September, 2014).
9. Mr. Janak Nanawati, Former member of Ahmedabad Traffic Advisory Committee (Interview date: 16 November, 2015).

10. Mr. M.S. Patel, former Deputy Commissioner and Transport Manager of the AMTS (Interview date: 2 October, 2015).
11. Dr. Manjula Subramaniam, Former Chief Secretary, Government of Gujarat and former Chairman of MEGA Co. Ltd. (Interview date: 19 November, 2014).
12. Mr. Pankaj Gandhi, Investor in buses, Chartered Logistics Expert (Interview date: 14 January, 2015).
13. Ms. Swati Buch, General Manager, GIDB Gandhinagar (Interview date: 31 October, 2015).
14. Mr. U.C. Padia, Dy. Municipal Commissioner, AMC, and Executive Director of Janmarg (Interview date: 14 and 15 August, 2013).
15. Mr. V.L. Patel, former Deputy Transport Manager (Interview date: 2 October, 2015).
16. Mr. Vijay Arya, Architect (Interview date: November 2014).
17. Mr. Vivek Ogra, ITS expert, Partner E&Y, Ahmedabad (Interview date: 14 September, 2014).

Bibliography

Agarwal, R. & Selen, W. (2011). Multi-dimensional nature of service innovation—Operationalisation of the elevated service offerings construct in collaborative service organisations. *International Journal of Production and Management, 31*(11), 1164-1192.

Ahmedabad JanMarg Ltd. (2008). *Bid evaluation document,* Ahmedabad.

Ahmedabad JanMarg Ltd. (2009). *RFP for low floor CNG bus and standard bus.*

Ahmedabad. Ahmedabad Municipal Corporation. (2008). *BRTS tender documents.*

Akrich, M. (1992).The description of technical objects. In W. Bijker, & J. Law (Eds.), *Shaping technology/building society: Studies in socio-technical ch*ange. Cambridge: MIT Press.

Akrich, M., Callon, M., & Latour, B. (2002). The key to success in innovation: Part 1—The art of interessement. *International Journal of Innovation Management.*

Albury, D. (2005). Fostering innovation in public services. *Public money and management, 25*(1), 51-56.

Alderman, N., Ivory, C., McLoughlin, I., & Vaughan, R. (2014). What makes a good project? Project management as a problem of translation. *9th EURAM Conference.* Liverpool: Newcastle University.

AMC (2006a). *Detail project report on bus rapid transit system.* Ahmedabad: Ahmedabad Municipal Corporation.

AMC (2006b, February). *JanMarg, Transforming Ahmedabad.* Retrieved August 2015, from Ahmedabadbrts.org: http://www.ahmedabadbrts.org/web/CM_Msg.html

AMC (2008). *Comprehensive mobility plan and bus rapid transit: Plan phase II.* Ahmedabad: AMC. Retrieved March 5, 2017, from http://www.ahmedabadbrts.org/web/images/Executive%20 Summary_ABRTS%20Phase-2.pdf

AMC, CoE-UT CEPT University (2008, May). Issues of CNG *vs.* Deisel. *Presentation to Supreme Court Commitee.*

AMTS (1996). *Feasibility of operating buses in exclusive lane on Ashram Road,* Ahmedabad (Unpublished). Pallavan Transport Company Ltd.

Andreasen, T.E. & Jensen, M.M. (2010). Design methods in practice–Beyond the 'systemic' approach of Pahl & Beitz. *International Design Conference — Design 2010.*

ANT and Inscriptions. (2015). Retrieved October 12th, 2015, from Actor network theory: https://actornetwork.wordpress.com/2009/08/21/ant-and-inscriptions/

Ardila, A. & Gomez (2004). *Transit planning in Curitiba and Bogotá: Roles in interaction, risk and change.* MIT.

Arnaboldi, M. & Spiller, N. (2011). Actor network theory and stakeholder collaboration: A case of cultural district. *Tourism Management, 2*(3), 641-654.

Barnes, M. (1969). *Time and money in contract control.* Course developed for University of Manchester, Manchester.

Bettencourt, Lobo & Strumsky (2007, February). Invention in the city: Increasing returns to patenting as a scaling function of metropolitan size. *Research Policy, 36*(1), 107-120. Retrieved January 2016, from http://www.sciencedirect.com/science/article/pii/S0048733306001661

(2012). *Bogota, Colombia Bus Rapid Transit Project—Transmilenio.* Special unit for South—South Cooperation. Retrieved from http://www.esc-pau.fr/ppp/documents/featured_projects/colombia_bogota.pdf

Briers, M. & Chua, W.F. (2011). The role of actor-network and boundary objects in management accounting change: A field study of an implementation of activity-based costing. *Accounting Organisations and Society*, 237-269.

Callon, M. (1986). Some elements of a sociology of translation: Domestication of the scallops and the fishermen of St. Brieuc Bay. In J. Law & J. Law (Ed.), *Power, action and belief: A new sociology of knowledge?* (pp. 196-233). London: Routledge & Kegan Paul.

Callon, M. (1987). Society in the making: The study of technology as a tool for sociological analysis. In W.E. Bijker, T.P. Hughes & T. Pinch (Eds.), *The Social Construction of Technological Systems* (pp. 83-103). MIT Press, Cambridge, MA.

Callon, M. (1991). Techno-economic networks and irreversibility. In L. John & J. Law (Ed.), *A sociology of monsters: Essays on power, technology and domination* (pp. 132-161). London: Routledge.

Callon, M. & Law, J. (1988). Engineering and sociology in a military aircraft project: A network analysis of technological change. *Social Problems, 35*(3), 284-297.

Carey, B. (2013). *Artifacts 'scripts' and the performer-developer.* Sydney: Faculty of Arts and Sciences.

Carroll, N. (2014). Actor-network theory: A bureaucratic view of public service innovation. In Tatnall, *Technological advancements and the impact of actor-network theory.* IGI Global.

Carroll, N., Richardson, I. & Whelan, E. (2012). Service science: An actor-network theory approach. *International Journal of Actor-Network Theory and Technological Innovation*, 51-69.

CEPT & GIDB (n.d.). *Ahmedabad bus rapid transit system—Vehicle technology.* Retrieved from Scribed.com: http://www.scribd.com/doc/89641972/01-Vehicle-Technology#scribd

CEPT, AMC, AUDA, GIDB. (2005, December). *Ahmedabad bus rapid transit system.* Retrieved August 2015, from ahmedabadbrts.org: http://www.ahmedabadbrts.org/web/images/04.Bus%20Station%20Design.pdf

Cervero, R. (2013). *Bus rapid transit (BRT): An efficient and competitive mode of public transport.* Berkeley, USA: ACEA. Retrieved March 5, 2017, from https://www.acea.be/uploads/publications/20th_SAG_HR.pdf

Chandran, R. (2010, July). *Urban transport debate: Is BRTS the answer?* Retrieved from livemint: http://www.livemint.com/Politics/rmrv69KmokVhBrcyee7nHM/Urban- transport-debate-Is-BRTS-the-answer.html

CoE-UT (2013). *Integrated transit for Ahmedabad.* CEPT.

CoE-UT, CEPT University (2013). *Simulation modelling—BRTS Network: A Case of Ahmedabad* (Unpublished). Ahmedabad.

CoE-UT, CEPT University (2014). *Monthly Progress Report on BRTS.* Ahmedabad: Ahmedabad Janmarg Limited (AJL).

Cresswell, K.M., Worth, A. & Sheikh, A. (2010). Actor-network theory and its role in understanding the implementation of information technology developments in healthcare. *BMC Medical Informatics and Decision Making, 10*(1), 67.

Dapice, D., Gomez-Ibanez, J. A. &Thanh, N.X. (2010). Ho Chi Minh City: The Challenges of Growth. *United Nations Development Programme in Vietnam*. UNDP. Retrieved from http://www.undp.org/content/dam/vietnam/docs/Publications/24699_20911_HCM_C hallenges_of_growth.pdf

Delhi Metro Rail Co. (2016). *Delhi Metro Annual Report 2015-16*. DMRC.

Deng, T. & Nelson, J. (2010). Recent developments in bus rapid transit: A review of the literature. *Transport Reviews,* Vol. 31, 69-96.

Desh Gujarat. (2009). Retrieved from A BRTS trial run experience in Ahmedabad: http://deshgujarat.com/2009/08/01/a-brts-trial-run-experience-in-ahmedabad/

Dimitrious, H.T., Low, N., Sturup, S., Zembri, G., Campagnac, E., Kaparos, G. & Petterson, F. (2014, Decemeber 1st). What constitutes a 'successful' mega transport project? *Planning Theory and Practice,* Vol. 15, No. 3, 389-430. Retrieved from tandfonline.com: http://www.tandfonline.com/doi/pdf/10.1080/14649357.2014.935084

Dimitrious, H.T., Low, N., Sturup, S., Zembri, G., Campagnac, E., Kaparos, G. & Petterson, F. (2014, Decemeber 1st). What constitutes a 'successful' mega transport project? *Planning Theory and Practice,* Vol. 15, No. 3, 389-430. Retrieved from tandfonline.com: http://www.tandfonline.com/doi/pdf/10.1080/14649357.2014.935084

Dwiartama, A. & Rosin, C. (2014). Exploring agency beyond humans: the compatibility of actor-network theory (ANT) and resilience thinking. *Ecology and Society, 19*(3).doi:http://dx.doi.org/10.5751/ES-06805-190328

Dym. C. (1994). *Engineering Design: A Synthesis Views*. Cambidge University.

EMBARQ; SIBRT; Bus Rapid Transit (2015, August). *Global BRT Data*. Retrieved August 2015, from brtdata.org: http://brtdata.org/

Federal Transit Authority (2007). *Bus Rapid Transit*. Retrieved 2010, from http://www.fta.dot.gov/assistance/technology/research_4240.html.

Gautam, I.P. (2010). *Organising existing para transit to work as feeder for Janmarg*. Ahmedabad: AMC.

Gautam, I. P., Swamy, H. M., Lokre, A. & Arya, V. (2014). *Innovations in Designs—Ahmedabad Bus Rapid Transit System.* Ahmedabad: mapinpub.

GIDB (2005). *DPR for Ahmedabad Metro.* GIDB.

Global Mass Transit (2010, May 1). *Delhi Metro Setting an Example in Media*. Retrieved April 2015, from globalmasstransit.net: http://www.globalmasstransit.net/archive.php?id=2946

GoI (2005). *Jawaharlal Nehru National Urban Renewal Mission.* Delhi: Government of India, Ministry of Urban Development.

Greenhalgh, C. & Rogers, M. (2007). *Trade Marks and Performance in UK Firms.* DIME.

Grossman, N. (n.d.). *Curitiba Bus Rapid Transit System.* Retrieved February 15, 2015, from Project for Public Spaces: http://placemaking.pps.org/great_public_spaces/one?public_place_id=613

Hartley, J. (2006). *Innovation and Its Contribution to Improvement: A Review for Policy-Makers, Policy Advisers, Managers and Researchers.* Warwick Business School. London: Department for Communities and Local Government.

Heeks, R. & Stanforth, C. (2015). Technological change in developing countries: opening the black box of process using actor-network theory. *Development Studies Research, 2*(1), 33-55.doi:10.1080/21665095.2015.1026610

Hertog, D. (2000). Knowledge-intensive business services as co-producers of innovation. *International Journal of Innovation Management*, 491-528.

Hilpinen, R. (2011). From nature facts to artifacts. University of Miami.

JanMarg, CEPT. (2015). *Monthly Report—BRTS User Satisfaction Survey.* JanMarg.

Jnnurm.nic. (2015, December). *JnNURM.* Retrieved from UIG Overview: http://jnnurm.nic.in/wp-content/uploads/2011/01/UIGOverview.pdf

Kably, L. (2017, July 28). Equal opportunity policy must for cos. *Times of India*. Retrieved from https://timesofindia.indiatimes.com/business/india-business/equal-opportunity- policy-must-for-cos/articleshow/59799180.cms

Kittelson & Associates (2003). Transit capacity and quality of service manual (TCQSM).In *TCRP 100.*Transportation Research Board.

Kliem, R. & Ludin, I. (1992). *The People Side of Project Management.* Gower Publishing Company.

Kocabili, A.B., Gemainboeck, P., Saunders, R. & Dong, A. (2011). Towards a relational approach to design process. *45th Annual Conference of the Architectural Science Association.* Sydney: The University of Sydney.

Latour, B. (1987). *Science in action: How to follow scientists and engineers through society.* Cambridge, Massachusetts, USA: Harvard University Press.

Latour, B. (1991). Technology is society made durable. In J. Law (Ed.), *A Sociology of Monsters: Essays on Power, Technology and Domination* (pp. 103-131). London: Routledge.

Latour, B. (1992). Where are the missing masses? The sociology of a few mundane artifacts. In W. Bijker & J. Law (Eds.), *In Shaping Technology-Building Society. Studies in Sociotechnical Change* (pp. 225-259). Cambridge: MIT Press.

Latour, B. (2005). *Reassembling the Social: An Introduction to Actor–Network Theory.* New York, USA: Oxford University Press.

Latour, B. (2015, September). *Gender and Technology.* Retrieved September 15, 2015, from gender-technology.tumblr: http://gender-technology.tumblr.com/post/44222927077/latour-where-are-the-missing-masses

Latour, B. & Callon, M. (1981). Unscrewing the bigleviathans: How actors macro structure in reality and how sociologist help them to do so. (K. Knoor & A. Cicourel, Eds.). *Advances in Social Theory and Methodology: Toward an Integration of Micro and Macro Sociologies*, 277-303.

Latour, B. & Johnson, J. (1988). Mixing humans with non-humans: Sociology of a door-closer. (L. Star, Ed.) *Social Problems*, 298-310.

Law, J. (1999). *Traduction/Trahison: Notes on ANT.* Retrieved January 25, 2017, from Centre for Science Studies — Lancaster University: http://www.comp.lancs.ac.uk/sociology/papers/Law-Traduction-Trahison.pdf

Law, J. (2010). On the methods of long distance control: Vessels, navigation, and the Portuguese route to India. *Heterogeneities DOT net.* Retrieved from http://www.heterogeneities.net/publications/Law1986MethodsofLongDistanceContro l.pdf

Law, J. (2010). On the Methods of Long Distance Control: Vessels, Navigation, and the Portuguese Route to India. *Heterogeneities DOT net*. Retrieved from http://www.heterogeneities.net/publications/Law1986MethodsofLongDistanceContro l.pdf

Lawer, D.U. (2005). Interoganisational standards, managing web services specifications for flexible supply chain. Physica Verlag, A Springer Company.

Levinson, H., Zimmerman, S., Clinger, J., Rutherford, S., Smith, R.L., Cracknell, J. & Soberman, R. (2003). *TCR Preport 90: Bus rapid transit, volume 1: Case studies in bus rapid transit.* Washington DC: TCRP, TRB.

Lopez, O.S. (2013, August). *Metropolis in Motion: Urban mobility ANT the Politics of Infrastrucutre in Marcelo Ebrard's Mexico City (shortdraft).* Retrieved March 5, 2017, from http://www.rc21.org/conferences/berlin2013/RC21-Berlin-Papers-7/21-1-OSosa_RC21_SHORTVERSION.pdf

Lundvall, B.A. (2009). Why The New Economy Is a Learning Economy. In W. Drachsler, R. Kattel & E.S. Reinert, *Techno-Economic Paradigms: Essays in Honour of Carlota Perez* (pp. 221-237). Anthem Press.

Mahadevia, D., Joshi, R. & Datey, A. (2013). *Promoting low carbon tranport in India: Low-carbon mobility in India and the challenges of social inclusion bus rapid transit (BRT) case studies in India.* Federal Ministry for the Environment, Nature, Conversation and Nuclear Safety.

Malaysian Science and Technology Information Centre (MASTIC). (2012). *National Survey of Innovation.* Uni-Technologies Sdn. Bhd (UTSB) Universiti Teknologi, Ministry of Science, Technology and Innovation, Malaysia (MOSTI. Skudai, Johor: Malaysian Science and Technology Information Centre (MASTIC).

Markus, L. & Robey, D. (1988). *Information and Technology and Organisational Change: Causal Structure in Theory and Research.* Management Science.

MEGA (2015). *Detailed Project Report for Ahmedabad Metro Rail Project (Phase-I).* MEGA.

Mehta, R. (2002). *History, Politics and Technology of CNG-Diesel Bus Switch in Delhi.* Delhi: Delhi Transport Corporation.

Metrobits (2014-15). *World Metro Database.* Retrieved September 2015, from metrobits.org: http://mic-ro.com/metro/table.html

Metrobits (2016, December 1). *World Metro Database*. Retrieved from Metrobits.org: http://mic-ro.com/metro/table.html

Miller, M.A. (2011). State and federal project development procedures for bus rapid transit: Managing differences and reducing implementation delays. *California PATH Research Report.*

Ministry of Road Transport and Highways (2012). *Road Transport Year Book* (*2011-12*). Transport Research Wing, Ministry of Road Transport and Highways, Government of India.

MoRTH (2019). *Road Transport Year Book 2018-19.* New Delhi: Ministry of Road Transport and Highways.

Ministry of Urban Development (2008). *Model Contract for City Bus Private Operations-Gross Cost (Volume II).* Retrieved February 2017, from http://moud.gov.in/upload/uploadfiles/files/Model GrossCost.pdf

Mohan, D. (n.d.). Public transportation systems for urban area—A brief review. *Transportation Research and Injury Prevention Programme.* Indian Institute of Technology, Delhi.

Moldaschl, M. (2010). *Why Innovation Theories make no Sense.* Chemnitz University of Technology, Department of Innovation Research and Sustainable.

Moore, C.F. (2005). Breakthrough innovations and continuous improvement: Two different models of innovative processes in the public sector. *Public Money and Management, 25*, 43-50.

Mulgan, G. (2014). *Innovation in the Public Sector: How can Public Organisations Better Create, Improve and Adapt?* London: Nesta.

National Transport Development Policy Committee (2014). *India Transport Report: Moving India to 2032 (Volume II)—Part I.* Routledge.

Nelson, R.R. (2005). Project perspectives: Evaluating project success, failure and everything in between. *MIS Quarterly Executive,* Vol. 4, No. 3.

Nimmo, R. (2011). Actor-network theory and methodology: Social research in a more-than-human world. *Methodological Innovations, University of Manchester*, 108-119.

OECD (2014). Building organisational capacity for public sector innovation. Paris: Innovating the Public Sector: From Ideas to Impact. doi:http://dx.doi.org/10.1787/9789264013100-en

Paul, J. (2012, October 3). *Parallel Routes can Derail Metro, BRTS efficacy*. Retrieved from Times of India: http://timesofindia.

indiatimes.com/city/ahmedabad/Parallel-routes- can-derail-metro-BRTS-efficacy/articleshow/16647701.cms

Pel, B. (2012). Beyond 'resistance to change': Interference management in system innovation. *3rd International Conference on Sustainability Transitions.* Copenhagen: Technical University of Denmark.

Pratham, P. (2014). *Urbanisation, City Size and Labour Productivity—Revisiting Optimal City Size Argument.* Ahmedabad: Unpublished dissertation.

Rhodes, D. (2005, January). *http://jorhodes.blogspot.in/.* Retrieved from http://jorhodes.blogspot.in/2005/01/chapter-five-methodology.html

Rhodes, J. (2009). *Using Actor-Network Theory to Trace An ICT (Telecenter): Implementation Trajectory in an African Women's Micro-Enterprise Development Organisation.* USC Annenberg School for Communication.

Ricci, A. (2006). Agent & Artifact (A & A): Artifact-based environment for MAS. *EMSE.*

Ritzer, G. (2005). *A Encyclopedia of Social Theory.* SAGE Publications. Retrieved from http://www.sagepub.com/:http://www.sagepub.com/sites/default/files/upm- binaries/5222_Ritzer Entries_beginning_with_A[1].pdf

Roger, A., Richard, B., Stephen, G., & Tony, T. (2010, May). *Success and Failure in Urban Transport Infrastructure Projects*. London, UK.

Roychowdhury, A. (2010). *CNG Programme in India: The Future Challenges*. (p. 6). Center for Science and Environment.

Schumpeter, J. A. (1939). *Business Cycles—A Theoretical, Historical and Statistical Analysis of the Capitalist Process.* New York: McGraw-Hill Book Company.

Scott-Smith, T. (2013). The least provocative path: An ANT lens on development project formation and dissolution. *Working Paper, 3*. Manchester: Centre for Development Informatics, University of Manchester.

Shiga, J. (2007). Translations: Artifacts from an actor-network perspective. *Artifact, 1*(1), 40-55.

Singh, G. (2012, March 18). *Bus Rapid Transit BRT in Delhi — Who Failed Whom*. Retrieved June 2015, from http://delhigreens.

com:http://delhigreens.com/2012/03/18/bus-rapid-transit-brt-in-delhi-who-failed-whom/

Sinha, S. (2019). *BRT Governance and Challenges—A Case of Indian Cities.* Ahmedabad: VREF Research Synthesis Project, Governance of Metropolitan Transport.

Soderstorm, O. (2017). Mobilities. In M. Jayne & K. Ward, *Urban Theory—New Critical Perspectives* (pp. 193-204). Routledge.

Sorensen, E. & Torfing, J. (2012). Introduction collaborative innovation in the public sector. *The Innovation Journal: The Public Sector Innovation Journal, 17*(1), 2. Retrieved from http://www.innovation.cc/volumes-issues/intro_eva_sorensen_torfing_17v1i1.pdf

Swamy, H.M. (2010). *Transfering Ownership to Ahmedabad-Jan, the People of Ahmedabad.* Retrieved August 20, 2015, from slideshare.net/EMBARQNetwork: http://www.slideshare.net/EMBARQNetwork/transferring-ownership-to-ahmedabadjan-the-people-of-ahmedabad

Swamy, H.M. (2011, May). *Ahmedabad Bus Rapid Transit System.* Retrieved from Slideshare: http://www.slideshare.net/sibrt/ahmedabad-bus-rapid-transit-system

Swamy, H.M. (2014). *JanMarg BRTS—Ahmedabad Bus Rapid Transit System.* Retrieved August 2015, from http://www.unescap.org/:http://www.unescap.org/sites/default/files/4.2%20 Institutional%20issues%20and%20 coordination%20in%20 sustainable%20transport%20-%20CEPT.pdf

Swamy, H.M., Lokre, A., Sinha, S. & Daftardar, C. (2015). Bus rapid transit systems: Global trends and Indian experiences. In D.M. Ramachandran, *Reforming Urban Transport in India—Issues and Best Practices* (pp. 193-236). Copal Publishing.

Swamy, H., & Sinha, S. (2014). Urban transport developments in India under NUTP and JnNURM. *John Diandas Memorial Lecture.* Colombo: Research Gate.

Taiyab, N. (2008, November). *Transportation in Mega—Cities: A Local Issue, A Global Question.* Retrieved from http://www.bu.edu/:http://www.bu.edu/pardee/files/documents/BU- Pardee-Policy-Paper-004-Megacities.pdf

The Energy and Resource Institute (2004). *Fuel Choices for Transport and the Environment.* New Delhi: TERI.

Thomos, E. (2001). *Presentation at Institute of Transportation Engineers Meeting*. Chicago.

Valderrama, A. (2010). How do we co-produce urban transport systems and thecity? The case of Transmilenio and Bagota. In *Urban Assesmblages, How Actor Network Theory Changes Urban Studies* (pp. 123-138). Routledge. Retrieved from https://books.google.co.in/books?hl=en&lr=&id=F2P0TYWNZKUC&oi=fnd&pg=PP2&dq=Urban+Assemblages+%2B+Valderrama+A.+2009&ots=UamL3Bj8iq&sig=- 6_eEXwTCUM4F2fXktN-z7tDlAM#v=onepage&q=Valderrama&f=false

Walsham, G. (1997). Actor-network theory and IS research: Current status and future prospects. *Information Systems and Qualitative Research*. doi:10.1007/978-0-387- 35309-8_23

Watson,V. (2016, December 6th). Shifting Approaches to Planning Theory: Global North and South. *Urban Planning, 1*(4), 32-41. doi:10.17645/up.v1i4.727

Wright, W. & Hook, L. (2007). *Bus Rapid Transit Planning Guide.* Retrieved from https://nbrti.org/docs/pdf/ITDP%20BRT%20Planning%20Guide.pdf

Zimmerman, S.L. & Levinson, H. (2007). Vehicle selection for BRT: Issues and options. *Journal of Public Transportation*. Retrieved from National BRT Institute: http://www.nbrti.org/docs/pdf/JPT_Vehicle_Image.pdf

Index